Helen Reynolds is an internationally known
management consultant in the areas of leadership,
time management, and communications.
She is listed in *Who's Who in Training and Development*
and in the *Organizational Development Network*.

Mary E. Tramel is a writer and consultant
in the areas of communications, time management,
and modern office procedures. Her writings
have appeared in publications in the United States
and Canada.

Both authors write from a rich background
of personal experience and knowledge. Their contact
with executives in middle management and up
has made possible the proven practicality of the
contents of this book.

Executive Time Management

Helen Reynolds & Mary E. Tramel

EXECUTIVE TIME MANAGEMENT

Getting 12 Hours' Work
out of an 8-Hour Day

A SPECTRUM BOOK

PRENTICE-HALL, INC., Englewood Cliffs, N.J. 07632

Library of Congress Cataloging in Publication Data

REYNOLDS, HELEN
   Executive time management.

   (A Spectrum Book)

   Includes bibliographical references and index.
     1. Time allocation. 2. Management. I. Tramel,
Mary E., joint author. II. Title.
HD38.R44   658.4   78-27645
ISBN 0-13-294371-9
ISBN 0-13-294355-7 pbk.

Editorial/production supervision
and interior design by Claudia Citarella
Cover design by Len Leoni, Jr.
Manufacturing buyer: Cathie Lenard

© 1979 by Prentice-Hall, Inc.,
Englewood Cliffs, N.J. 07632

A SPECTRUM BOOK

Printed in the United States of America

10 9 8 7 6 5

PRENTICE-HALL INTERNATIONAL, INC., London
PRENTICE-HALL OF AUSTRALIA PTY. LIMITED, Sydney
PRENTICE-HALL OF CANADA, LTD., Toronto
PRENTICE-HALL OF INDIA PRIVATE LIMITED, New Delhi
PRENTICE-HALL OF JAPAN, INC., Tokyo
PRENTICE-HALL OF SOUTHEAST ASIA PTE. LTD., Singapore
WHITEHALL BOOKS LIMITED, Wellington, New Zealand

Preface

Executive Time Management deals with the peculiar kinds of time-use problems executives face. Executives at all levels of business and the professions can find help for everyday time problems through the many practical suggestions found in the text.

Chapter by chapter the text deals with the kinds of things executives do—planning, paperwork, deciding, writing, conversing, conferring, leading—and presents productive procedures for each of these areas of executive activity.

Many time management tools are presented and their use explained step by step. Executives will discover these time tools easy to adapt for their own use and the use of their support staffs.

The writing style is conversational and the book is well organized and easy to follow. The text is based not only on theory but on practical experience: Time management methods outlined here are successfully being used by executives in all fields. We gratefully acknowledge the willingness of the many managers who have attended our seminars and shared their successes with us. The text is really a compilation of the procedures they are finding to be workable.

Carol Walczak created the octopus drawings scattered throughout the text. Her tongue-in-cheek parallelism of some executive and octopus traits are germane to points made in the text. We acknowledge and appreciate her work.

Helen Reynolds

Mary E. Tramel

Introduction

BE WISE ABOUT TIME

And God called the light Day, and the darkness he called Night. And the evening and the morning were the first day. (Gen. 1:5)

Ever since the first night and day time has continued on. Man has tried to capture it on calendars, to measure it by the ticktock of the clock, to extend it by daylight savings time, to speed it up, to slow it down, to spend it, to save it, to budget it. Man has discovered time to be elusive, to be relative, to be equitably distributed without discrimination, to be spendable although it cannot be bought, to be friend, to be foe, to be constant and sure, to be displaceable but not replaceable, to be usable.

Time never stands still—although it may seem to. It never flies—although we are certain it does. We all have time—although we complain bitterly there is no time.

Time passed is history. Time to come is only assumption. Now is all the time we have. Time is here. Time is now. Even as you read this sentence, the time it takes is vanishing like a vapor. An old English proverb says, "Time and tide wait for no man." Man can manipulate the atom, but he cannot harness the tide nor inhibit the flow of time.

Nevertheless, man can use time. And the first step in using time is to realize it is as constant and steady as the tide. Scientists, realizing the nature of the tide, have long looked for a feasible way to use it to create energy. In the same way successful executives look for ways to use the constant, steady time to reach personal and organizational goals.

In so doing they have also come to the realization that, like the water of the ocean, time is displaceable. A child playing on the beach has a bucket filled to the brim with sea water. He dumps a shovelful of sand into the bucket and some of the water splashes out. Similarly, you have an eight-hour workday filled with time. If into that workday you dump one hour of dictating to your secretary, what happens? One hour of time vanishes out of your workday. The secret to controlling time, then, lies in controlling the activities you displace it with.

Another thing about time is that it will control you if you don't control it. You can neglect writing to a friend or making a phone call. You can neglect getting started on a report that was due yesterday. You can neglect almost anything you should do and you will not feel as guilty as you will when you know you have carelessly wasted time. Some people feel so guilty when they have wasted time that they spend hours fretting about it, making excuses, and accomplishing nothing. Others feel so guilty that they immediately busy themselves with whatever comes to mind—not wasting another second, or so they think. But eventually they begin to wonder why they have not been able to accomplish more, "as hard as I've worked all these years." They make time their taskmaster. Instead of using time to accomplish their goal, they have made their goal *not wasting time.*

These people fail to realize that it's really okay to waste time, if you waste it purposefully. Time cannot make you feel guilty for taking a respite if it is part of a well-thought-out plan to accomplish a goal. Millions in vacation pay are paid to workers every year, not only because the unions demand it, but because it's profitable to business for workers to take a breather once a year.

Big business and individuals control time to the extent that they control their use of it.

Contents

   xi

6

A Time to Write   70

7

A Time to Converse   90

8

A Time to Confer   114

9

A Time to Lead   128

10

A Time To Take Stock   153

Executive Time Management

1

Controlling Time Wisely to Satisfy Life Values

TAKE TIME TO THINK AND PLAN

Well over two hundred years ago Benjamin Franklin wrote:

> If you want to enjoy one of the greatest luxuries in life, the luxury of having enough time, time to rest, time to think things through, time to get things done and know you have done them to the best of your ability, remember there is only one way. Take enough time to think and plan things in the order of their importance. Your life will take on a new zest, you will add years to your life, and more life to your years. Let all your things have their places. Let each part of your business have its time.

The people of Ben Franklin's day complained of not having enough time. But wise Ben had the answer to the dilemma, and successful people find it to be the right answer even today: *Take time to think and plan things in the order of their importance.*

Taking time to think and plan things is as vital on life's busy highway as waiting for the green light to enter one of California's freeways. It takes a little time at the beginning, but saves time later by helping to keep traffic tie-ups to a minimum.

THE FASTEST ROUTE TO SUCCESS

Follow the signposts for the fastest route to success.

Determine Values.   What are the things in life that mean most to you? Career? Health? Family relationships? Financial security? Recognition? Spiritual values? Write them down on paper.

Prioritize.   Put your values in the order of importance to you. On which of the values you have listed do you place the highest priority? What do you spend most of your free time thinking about, planning for, and doing? What excites and motivates you? Whatever it is, that is your

most important value and it will influence what you do with all your other values. If, after thinking this step through honestly, you don't like what it reveals, you may want to change where you are placing your priority. Your real values can be lost if you allow lesser values to take too large a share of your attention.

Chart.   Make a chart, first placing at the top your most important value. Under this, halfway down the page, list all your other important values, in order of priority, from left to right.

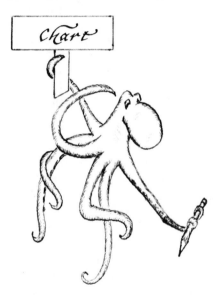

Establish Goals.   Now you are ready to establish long-range goals for each value. Begin with your primary value and set goals for it; then do the same for each of your other values. As you do, remember that your goals must always be subservient to your values. In other words, you should not have a goal under *career* that would hinder the value you

place on *family relationships.* For example, suppose you place a very high value on your marriage and you want nothing to hinder that relationship, not even your career. But you value your career also; you would like to be president of your company. However, to become president of your company would require certain sacrifices that would put a strain on your marriage. Perhaps you would have to live in a distant country apart from your spouse for long periods of time. If your spouse places the same value on your career as you do, the two of you might be able to work out a solution. But if a solution that is satisfactory to both of you cannot be worked out, you would be placing a lower value on your marriage than you have placed on your career if you pursued the goal to be president of your company. Be sure your goals are concrete and reachable.

As you go through life, your goals and even the priority order of your values may change. This is normal. It's a healthy sign that you are growing and reaching, not static and inflexible. Take time to rethink your values and goals at least yearly.

Establish Steps. For each long-range goal, establish a series of steps to bring you closer to realization of that goal. At this point you may not be able to foresee all the steps it will take to reach your goal, but list as many as you can. Establish a completion date for the first step and completion dates for as many subsequent steps as you can at this time.

Under *family relationships,* for example, you may have a goal to become a closer knit family than you are now. Perhaps each family member eats on the run and you seldom sit down to a meal together. A step might be to plan things so that the family can eat at least one meal together every day. Or, if under *spiritual values* one of your goals is for

you and your family to be more aware of blessings and more thankful for them, a step under this goal could be to have prayer before the meal you will eat together. Here is an opportunity to link steps under separate values; you will find many such opportunities to link steps.

Each time a step is accomplished, check it off and go to the next step. If you have not already done so, determine the completion date for that step and begin work on it. Determine new steps and change the steps you have already established as the current situation dictates. When you have reached your goal, establish a new goal under that value.

By now, if you have complied with the road signs, you will have a large chart of your values, goals, and steps set up like the example in Figure 1–1. After you have completed your chart, with all your goals and steps listed under each value, you may want to put it up on a wall of your

```
                 Most Important Value:  Financial Security

Goal:  To have six months' income in savings account

Steps:                                              Completion
   1.   Study present budget to cut down on expenses    Nov. 1
   2.   Make monthly deposits of $_____                start Dec. 1
   3.   Purchase high-interest, long-term notes



Value:  Career                    Value:  Family Relationships

Goal:  To be Pres. of Company     Goal:  To spend more time with family

Step 1:  Take adv. crse. in Bus. Adm.   Step 1:  Plan a family outing for
            - spring semester                    November 11
```

Figure 1–1. Goals

home study or workroom. Looking at it once in a while will help to keep you on course. And as you check off each step, you will have a feeling of accomplishment.

Some people prefer to list each value, along with the goals and steps pertaining to it, on a separate 5 by 8 card. The advantage of having a large chart is that you will look at it frequently. If you prefer to use cards, take them out and read them weekly. There is something about reading your goals regularly that establishes them in your subconscious and programs you for success.

FOR EVERYTHING THERE IS A SEASON

Does your chart look formidable—an impossibility to accomplish in one lifetime? If so, you probably feel like a giant octopus. The giant octopus has eight powerful arms, each provided with two rows of adhesive suckers. Like executives, octopuses live between rocks and hard places most of the time. Suppose you are a giant octopus and you have planted each arm on a different rock; each rock represents an area of your life that is demanding your attention and time. Now, imagine you have mysteriously lost the ability to release your arms. The more you try to pull them back, the tighter they stick. The tighter they stick, the more they pull away from you. Something has to give—and it's not going to be

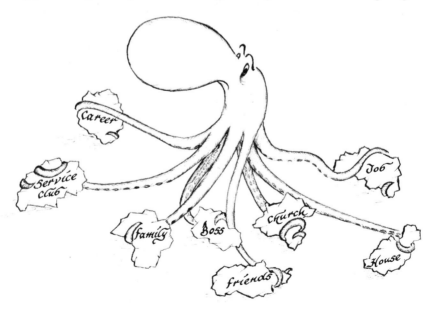

a rock! The moral: Before you plant your arms be sure you are planting them where you want them to be. And be sure you will be able to release them. An octopus uses only two arms to move ahead. While these are alternately planted and released, planted and released, the other arms flow free much like feelers. Sometimes an octopus stops and gathers all his arms about himself for protection.

You *can* accomplish everything on your big chart in a normal life span, and perhaps do more, if you know when to plant and when to release, when to feel your way and when to rest.

2

Wise Control
of Your 8-to-5 Time

To bring about change, whether it be a wiser use of time or a better functioning office staff, there must be a catalyst—an agent of change, something or someone injected into the situation to bring about the desired change.

If you want to change the way you use your time so that you will use it more wisely, you are the catalyst to bring about that desired change. If you want your organizational team to make wiser use of time, you must consciously put yourself into the arena as the catalyst that will bring about that desired change. If you are convinced your superior could use time more wisely, again you are the catalyst to try to bring about the change you desire in your superior. It is not likely that the change will occur unless you want it enough to be the agent to bring it about.

If you are going to be that all-important catalyst, it is important that you know yourself. A chef seasons the soup with herbs and spices. If he adds them in just the right combinations, in the right proportions, and at the right time, the result is a delicious blend of flavors. But if the chef doesn't know how herbs and spices will affect the soup, if he tosses them in at random, it is doubtful that the soup will be very tasty. Similarly, if you are going to put yourself into your job situation, into your boss's arena, or into your organization for the purpose of creating a change in the way time is used, you are going to have to know yourself.

KNOW YOURSELF

Here are some questions to ask yourself. Your frank answers will reveal thought and work habits that you need to be aware of in order to bring about a wiser use of time. There are no right or wrong answers to these questions. They are meant to help you analyze your habits, good or bad.

A. How organized are you?

1. Do you work at a cluttered desk? Or at an orderly desk with a place for everything and everything in its place?
2. Do you plan ahead?
3. Are you a list maker?
4. How much time do you spend on list making? Do you list only what you need to list to help you remember and keep on schedule? Do you spend so much time making lists that you don't have time left to do what you have listed? Do you avoid making lists altogether and try to keep mental notes that get all jumbled up in your mind and cause you to lose time trying to remember?
5. Do you do tasks in priority order?
6. Do you have many active interests? Or do you concentrate your efforts on a few vital ones?
7. Do you do everything you do with a purpose?
8. Have you learned how to say no?

B. What are your habits?

1. Are you a chronic complainer?
2. Do you begin each day with a conscious effort to be enthusiastic?
3. How punctual are you? Do you make an effort to get an early start?

4. Do you habitually comply with the status quo, or do you look for a better way?

5. Do you procrastinate?

6. Do you relegate and release?

C. What are your personality traits?

1. Are you an optimist or a pessimist?

2. Do you like to work with people, or do you prefer to work alone?

3. Do you have empathy? Can you see yourself and your position through the eyes of your superior? Through the eyes of your subordinates?

4. Are you a perfectionist, dotting every i and crossing every t?

5. Do you worry a lot?

6. Do you put off making decisions?

7. Are you aware of your personal rhythm? Do you know when your up cycle is likely to be and when you will be feeling down?

8. Are you a quick starter or a slow starter? Do you know your most creative time of day?

9. Are you motivated to change the way you use your time?

KNOW YOUR PURPOSE

Get out the organization chart for your organization or your division. If your organization doesn't have one, take time right now to sketch one.

At the very top of the page write in your organization's or division's reason for being, that is, its primary purpose. Unless you work for a bureaucracy that has outlived its purpose, you should have no difficulty in filling in the primary purpose. It is the reason you and everyone else in the organization were hired. It is either to sell a product or service or to administer a program.

There should be a line coming down from the primary purpose to the organization's chairman of the board or president, or if it's a division chart, to the division head. Now the lines continue down through various A-level executives to B-level managers, and on down through many assistants and other employees all with varying functions until they all converge on whoever is in the lowest position on the organization chart. Somewhere in this maze of organization is a rectangle with your name on it. Do you see it? Good! Keep your finger on it and consider for a moment the person down there at the bottom of the page. Suppose it is the file clerk. What is the file clerk's primary goal or purpose? To file papers? *No!* That may be a *function* of the position and a secondary reason why s/he was hired. But the organization does not exist for the *purpose* of filing papers. It exists for whatever the primary purpose at the top of the page is. If it were not for that goal there would be no organization and no file clerk. So the primary goal is as much the file clerk's primary purpose as it is top management's, regardless of what each actually does from day to day.

With this thought in mind, consider your own position. Your primary purpose is also to achieve the organization's or division's goal. The more you can contribute to the achievement of your organization's or division's goal, the more valuable you are. Your function may be to supervise x number of salesmen or department heads or to manage an office force—but that is not your primary purpose. In your thinking, always keep your function secondary to your primary purpose. It will save you years in your climb to career success.

The organization chart does tell you also, in a very general, comprehensive way, what your function (secondary purpose) is. Suppose you have been employed as Director of Purchasing and Stores for a large school district. It is your first day on the job and while you have a general idea of your area of responsibility, you need more specifics. So you look at the organization chart for the Business Division of which the Purchasing Department is a part. See Figure 2–1.

You discover from the organization chart:

1. Your primary purpose (to provide quality education)
2. Your area of responsibility (purchasing)
3. Who you report to (assistant superintendent—business)
4. Who reports to you (purchase order machine operator, buyers, secretary, purchasing clerks, storekeepers)
5. Who you cooperate with (shown by dotted lines: schools and their staffs, all other district-level divisions and departments, and their staffs)

Having found your place in the scheme of things, you lean back in your purchasing director's chair and contemplate your primary purpose, that of providing quality education for the pupils of the school district. In due time, someone places your job description before you. It

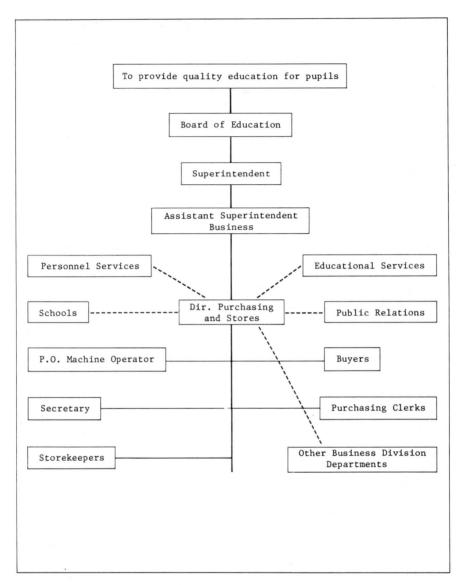

Figure 2–1. Plan of Organization

says: Under general direction shall administer an efficient centralized purchasing service and district warehouse operation for all schools, divisions, and departments of the district. Shall train personnel and perform other business activities as directed. This is followed by many Examples of Duties that describe your function in specific terms.

12

You realize that as you and your staff perform the functions listed on the job description you will be contributing to the school district's primary goal to provide quality education for pupils. But something is missing.

When you were interviewed for this position you were keenly aware of your division chief's interest in your innovative ideas for the purchasing department's role in the achievement of the district's primary goal. In fact, that seemed to be the reason you were chosen over other applicants. Yet, nowhere on the organization chart or the job description does it say that innovation is a part of your function. But it is, if you want to be a successful director of purchasing and stores. However, success does not come easily. It takes a great deal of agility of mind to juggle conformity with the leadership structure (organization chart), compliance with job specifications, other written and unwritten policies, and your own innovative ideas, without dropping one. But this is a skill you must learn in order to avoid getting tangled up in time-consuming matters that make no contribution to the achievement of the district's primary purpose.

KNOW HOW YOU ARE SPENDING YOUR TIME

Your value as an executive is measured in degrees of effectiveness. It is not so much how efficiently you perform your function as it is how effectively you move toward the attainment of the organization's primary goal.

Efficiency is doing the job right.
Effectiveness is doing the right job.

Peter F. Drucker, author of several management books, says in *The Effective Executive* that effective executives start out by finding where their time actually goes.[1]

To do this, you should keep a Time Record and Analysis for each day for a week. (See Figure 2–2.) Select a week that is normal, not one in which you will attend a convention or take some time off or in which some other unusual occurrence is expected.

1. Put the date at the top.

---

[1]Adapted from Peter F. Drucker, *The Effective Executive* (New York: Harper & Row, Publishers, Inc., 1966), p. 25. Copyright © 1966, 1967 by Peter F. Drucker. By permission of the publisher.

TIME RECORD AND ANALYSIS SHEET   Date:_____

Time	What I Did	1	2	3	Time	What I Did	1	2	3
7:00					2:30				
7:15					2:45				
7:30					3:00				
7:45					3:15				
8:00					3:30				
8:15					3:45				
8:30					4:00				
8:45					4:15				
9:00					4:30				
9:15					4:45				
9:30					5:00				
9:45					5:15				
10:00					5:30				
10:15					5:45				
10:30					6:00				
10:45					6:15				
11:00					6:30				
11:15					6:45				
11:30					7:00				
11:45					7:15				
12:00					7:30				
12:15					7:45				
12:30					8:00				
12:45					8:15				
1:00					8:30				
1:15					8:45				
1:30					9:00				
1:45					9:15				
2:00					9:30				
2:15					9:45				

Figure 2–2. Time Analysis

2. Enter on the appropriate line what you are doing every fifteen minutes during the day. (Yes, this will take time; but after you have made the analysis, it will save you many future productive hours.)

3. At the end of the day, and with all the hindsight you can muster, check each activity in Column 1, 2, or 3.

Column 1:   You did the right thing at the right time.

Column 2:   You did the right thing but at the wrong time. (Maybe something occurred later in the day that would have made it easier for you if you had waited until then to do it.)

Column 3:   You did the wrong thing (something that didn't have to be done at all—at least not by you).

A careful analysis of your daily charts over a week's time will give you a good idea of how you are spending your time. You may find that productive managerial hours are being displaced out of your workday in fifteen-minute segments devoted to such nonproductive tasks as sharpening pencils, adding figures, dictating routine correspondence, making copies, redoing tasks because of insufficient preplanning, and so forth. Perhaps, like the octopus, you should release some arms and get rid of some rocks, either by delegating to subordinates or relegating to file 13. Wise delegating as a time tool will be discussed in Chapter 9.

SPEND EXECUTIVE TIME MORE EFFECTIVELY

Plan your work and work your plan daily is good advice for the executive who wants to use time wisely. You should not only plan your work mentally, but also get your plan down on paper. This will help to keep you on target so you will not be sidetracked by lesser items coming to your attention during the day.

Figure 2–3 is a sample form for a daily work plan. Whatever format is used, it should be one that will stand out from other papers on your desk. If you normally have a lot of goldenrod paper on your desk, your Daily Organizer should be on blue or some color other than goldenrod. Don't throw these away at the end of the day, but save them in a loose-leaf binder. They will be invaluable to you later as you reschedule repetitive tasks.

HOW TO USE THE DAILY ORGANIZER

1. Establish a system for denoting priorities.

   Priority A = Must do today

   Priority B = Should do today

DAILY ORGANIZER   Date: _____

TO PHONE:

Person	Regarding	P

APPOINTMENTS:

When	Person and Place	Time

TO DO:

Task	P

TO FOLLOW UP:

Figure 2–3. Daily Organizer

Priority C = Could put off

Priority /D = Can delegate

2. In the *To Do* section, list your paperwork goals for today, assigning each one a priority, A, B, or C. If one of your goals can be delegated to an employee, list it as an A/D, B/D, or C/D. If, while you are doing paperwork, it is necessary for you to make a

phone call to clarify a point, make the phone call then, rather than listing it on the *To Phone* list. Preferably, you would have clarified all points before beginning the paperwork project by putting the phone call to clarify the point on a *To Phone* list prior to the time you plan to do the paperwork. If your concentration on the paperwork project is interrupted by having to make a phone call, you will lose valuable time.

3. In the *To Phone* section, list each person you plan to call that day and the subject. Again, assign a priority to each call.

4. In the *Appointments* section, list the time, the person you will be seeing, and the place (your office, appointee's office, or other). In the *Time* column put the maximum amount of your time you think this appointment warrants. A minute or two before that amount of time is used up, start to bring the conversation to a close. You will not always be able to do so, but with a time goal before you, you will find it easier to keep appointments from dragging on unnecessarily.

5. Appointments must be taken care of as they have been scheduled. However, on your *To Do* and *To Phone* lists, complete all A priorities before going to B priorities. Complete all B priorities before going to C priorities.

6. During the day enter any task or phone call on which you need to follow up in the *To Follow Up* section. Put down enough detail so you will know exactly where you have left off and what the next follow-up step is. Consider this section as you prepare your Daily Organizer for the next workday.

7. Schedule one hour of uncommitted time each day to take care of the unexpected. If you do not need the hour, use it to catch up on desk work.

Some Reasons Why Schedules May Not Work

You will find it nearly impossible to complete everything on your *To Do* list each day. The important thing is that what you do accomplish are your highest priorities. The reason you cannot accomplish the entire list could be any of the following:

1. You may be trying to accomplish too much.

2. You may not be ready to do some of the things you listed or your goal is not clearly formulated. Consequently, you are jumping into a task in the middle without sufficient analyzing of the task step by step.

3. You may not be paying attention to task priorities. Charles Schwab turned the unknown Bethlehem Steel Company into the biggest independent steel producer in the world in just five

years. How? Largely by following the advice of an efficiency expert named Ivy Lee. Lee advised Schwab to follow a simple routine every workday and to have his staff do the same. The routine: to write down the six most important things he had to do the next day, and then to arrange them in order of importance. The next day Schwab was to start on Number One and stay with it until the task was completed; then do Number Two, then Number Three, and so on. It didn't matter if all the tasks were not completed that day. Time was spent on the most important ones. After trying this system for a few weeks, Schwab thought it worked well enough to pay Lee $25,000 for his advice.[2]

4. You may be failing to complete decision-making tasks if you find it difficult to make a decision. Chapter 5 will help you over such an obstacle.

5. Due to a breakdown in communication, you may not have all the needed information to complete the task. See Chapter 9 for suggestions on working effectively with your professional staff.

6. Your self-discipline may be failing you and you are:

   ▶ Neglecting to plan because you are feeling pressured.

   ▶ Not staying with the task because you are finding it difficult or boring.

   ▶ Allowing a contrary desire to weaken your principal purpose.

7. You may lack self-confidence to achieve your goal.

[2]Frank Bettga, *How I Multiplied My Income and Happiness in Selling* (Englewood Cliffs, N.J.: Prentice-Hall, Inc., 1954).

8. You may be testing the water around the edges of a task instead of plunging in.

9. You may be dwelling on past failures instead of optimistically working toward success.

10. You may be thinking, *I probably won't finish it* instead of *I can and I will.*

3

A Time
to Plan

There is an old Spanish proverb that says, *If you build no castles in the air, you build no castles anywhere.* Most of us in the American culture were brought up to think of daydreaming as an unwise use of time. But successful executives find that controlled daydreaming is an absolute *must.* It is called *planning.* The higher up in their organization they are, the more time executives spend on planning. Edwin C. Bliss in his book, *Getting Things Done,* says that you need a game plan for your day. Otherwise, you will allocate your time to whatever happens to land on your desk. He says that without a plan you wind up dealing with problems instead of opportunities.[1]

Planning cuts down on unproductive activity and procrastination.

[1]Edwin C. Bliss, *Getting Things Done: The ABC's of Time Management* (New York: Charles Scribner's Sons, n.d.).

The process can be compared to looking through a cam
kinds of lenses: a wide-angle lens and a telescopic le

WIDE-ANGLE PLANNING

Wide-angle planning gives you the large picture. This is when you rethink your long-range goals and establish short-range objectives for them. This is a time to reminisce on the past: to learn from mistakes and build on successes. It's a time to explore ways to increase your personal contribution to the organization's goal. It's also a time to increase your professional awareness through study and reading of literature related to your field. Reserve an hour or two on your weekly schedule for wide-angle planning. If possible, do it away from your office where your thoughts will not be inhibited by the pressures of the day. Find a quiet place at home or some other spot where you can feel comfortable and relaxed.

Wide-angle planning is easy to neglect because it does not demand your attention. Don't neglect it. It's a wise investment of time that pays high dividends.

TELESCOPIC PLANNING

Telescopic planning zeroes in on specific problems and tasks. This is a time to:

- ▶ *Plan* your day using your Daily Work Organizer mentioned in Chapter 2.
- ▶ *Think* through people problems.
- ▶ *Schedule* time. The following guide is often used by managers when scheduling time:

    38% of time for problems that come up that day.

    40% of time for problems up to a week ahead.

    15% of time for problems from one week to one month ahead.

    5% of time for problems one to six months ahead.

    2% of time for problems six months to one year ahead.

Establish a quiet hour sometime during each workday for telescopic planning. Choose a time when you can have solitude, when you can give concentrated attention to your thoughts without being interrupted by phone, caller, or secretary. For some, this is the first hour of the day. If your day starts off with a bang the moment your office is open, you may want to come in an hour earlier, before the rush begins. If it's not possible to start early, find another time—either the last hour of the day, or just before or just after lunch. The point is to establish your own voluntary solitude for at least an hour each day. If possible, pick the same hour every day so people will get to know you are not available for that time. Don't be misled by the mistaken notion that executives should always be accessible. This idea has led to the open-door policy, which is an open invitation for corridor wanderers to drop in for a visit.

The next step is to find a place to do your telescopic planning. This could be your own office, provided you have someone who is skilled in keeping all distractions away from you for this time. However, if your office is too accessible, you may be able to find a secret hideout for your thinking time.

Don't be concerned about your superior's thinking you are wasting time because you are seemingly doing nothing. Your superior probably has a quiet hour too for his or her planning. And even if this is not the case, your effectiveness as a result of your planning time will soon convince your superior of the wisdom of your allocating such a time.

RECORD, MANAGE, AND CONSOLIDATE TIME

Peter Drucker says:

> This three-step process of recording time–managing time–consolidating time is the foundation of executive effectiveness.[2]

You already recorded time when you made your Time Analysis in Chapter 2. You have begun to manage your time if you relegated and released tasks that don't belong there. You should repeat this recording and managing of your time at least every six months. Unproductive activities have a way of creeping back into your schedule and you need to periodically search them out and dispose of them.

[2]Excerpt from Peter F. Drucker, *The Effective Executive* (New York: Harper & Row, Publishers, Inc., 1966), p. 25. Copyright© 1966, 1967 by Peter F. Drucker. By permission of the publisher.

After you have recorded and managed your time, you will know how much time you have left for tasks that only you can do. The problem is that this time is scattered in small segments throughout the day. Small bits of time, although they may add up to one or two hours, are not sufficient for most executive tasks. You can spend hours in fifteen-minute segments on a task that requires executive-level planning and never get it accomplished. What you need is a system for blocking time so you will have large chunks of it instead of small segments. Here are several ways you can accomplish this:

1. Work at home one day a week.
2. Schedule all meetings, conferences, problem-solving sessions, and the like for two days a week, say Monday and Friday. Set aside either the mornings or afternoons of Tuesday, Wednesday, and Thursday for executive tasks.
3. Schedule a daily work period at home in the morning, say an hour or hour and a half. This is better than taking work home to do in the evening. By the end of the day you are not as productive as you are earlier. Besides, the rest of the family are probably going about their own activities in the morning and would appreciate your attention more in the evening.
4. Consolidate phone calls. (See Chapter 7.)
5. Eat a late breakfast and work through the lunch hour.

Having scheduled some large blocks of time for executive planning, you need some tools to help you use this time wisely. Here are some that other top executives have found to be useful.

APPOINTMENT CALENDARS

Executives need to have three appointment calendars: a pocket calendar, a desk calendar, and a daily plan.

Pocket Calendar. Carry a small pocket calendar with you at all times. If it becomes necessary to make an appointment or schedule a meeting while you are away from your office, a glance at your pocket calendar will tell you what time you have available. Your desk calendar should remain at the office on your assistant's desk.

Cautions. (a) Be sure to schedule a few minutes (five at the most) once or twice a day for your assistant to coordinate the two calendars. (b)

Always make entries on both calendars in pencil. Then if revisions are necessary, the original entry can be erased and the revised entry written in its place.

Your pocket calendar will not carry as much information as your desk calendar. All that is needed is the name of the person or persons you have an appointment with entered on the appropriate time line. This calendar is simply to tell you that that particular time is taken and by whom. It saves your having to phone your office for this information when you want to schedule another appointment.

Desk Calendar.   Your desk calendar, which is kept by your assistant, will contain on the appropriate date and time line:

▶ Person or persons appointment is with.
▶ Place of meeting.
▶ Subject of meeting (reason for appointment).

Your assistant uses this calendar to schedule appointments for you as requests for appointments come in. S/he will know how much time you have available and when. That is why it is important that you allow your assistant to have your pocket calendar once or twice a day so both calendars can be kept current.

Daily Plan.   Your third calendar, the daily plan, is the one that will save you time and make your appointments productive. It is prepared by your assistant first thing in the morning before your arrival or last thing the day before. It contains: time, name(s), subject, and any other pertinent information you need to facilitate the appointment. The following are typical entries on the daily plan:

10 A.M.   Mr. Burton—to discuss your participation in Civic Fund. (You told him previously you would consider serving on the Board of Directors.)

11 A.M.   Mrs. Goodal of Chamber of Commerce—to discuss upcoming membership drive. (The strategy outline you requested is being typed now.)

1 P.M.   Mr. Brown and Mr. White of Black and Co.—to discuss architectural services. (Their correspondence is attached.)

Your daily plan can be typed on 8½ by 11 paper or on 5 by 8 cards; the date could be used for the heading. You can use this daily plan to complete your Daily Work Organizer (Figure 2–3).

Pointers for Calendaring

1. Avoid too tight scheduling. This has a tension-building effect on you and your visitors. Time pressure cuts down on your effectiveness.

2. Have your assistant post regular recurring meetings at least three months in advance so that you don't get double-scheduled for those times.

3. Schedule long-winded callers at psychologically strategic times—just before their lunch time, just before their quitting time, just before a meeting. This will give you an excuse to bring the appointment to a close.

4. Have an understanding with your assistant that s/he is to call or come in to remind you of another appointment. Then say, "We'll only be another three minutes"—and hope that your guest will take the hint.

5. Consider going to an employee's office instead of having the employee come to yours. This will give you a chance to get out and see what's going on and make it easier for you to close the interview.

6. If a person is late for an appointment, tell the caller your time constraint and ask if the business can be finished within that period or if the appointment should be rescheduled. One late appointment can put you behind for the remainder of the day.

7. Remember that other people's time is important to them. If a delay on your part is absolutely necessary, have your assistant or someone else explain the delay, offer some refreshments, and, most important, check back with the visitor frequently.

8. Blocking time is an excellent technique for assuring completion of high-priority projects. When laying out your weekly schedule, block out enough time for high-priority projects that require a lot of time. Schedule enough time in a block so you can build up momentum. Reserve certain days of the week for such projects. When you leave a project unfinished, make a note of what the next step is so you will not have to waste time reviewing when you return to the project. (See Figure 4–2 and explanation of Next Step Slip in Chapter 4.)

TASK CHARTING

Task charting is a system to streamline the organization of specific tasks. Given a task to do:

1. Identify the task goal. Determine exactly what is to be accomplished.
2. Think through all necessary steps to complete the task. Try thinking backwards, from completed goal to beginning of task, to avoid leaving out essential steps.
3. Arrange the steps in logical order. Weigh alternatives. Ask yourself, "What if I did this before that?" "Would it save time if I did that before this?"
4. After the steps are arranged in logical order, assign a symbol to each step. Here are five basic symbols. You may want to think of others, depending on the task you have to do.

-/-   Go or Stop
      (Appears at both beginning and end)

?   Input
      (Stands for ingredients necessary for success of project)

!   Imperative
      (Used when action is needed to complete a step. With goal in mind and the necessary input at hand, there's no reason to stall!)

*   Decision
      (You need to make a decision.)

Example of Task Charting

Task	To determine office budget for coming fiscal year.
Identify task goals	To come up with dollar amount needed for supplies and equipment for next fiscal year; and to prepare the budget in typewritten form.
Think of necessary steps to complete task	Find out if there will be any change in company letterhead (I heard there might be).
	Find out how much of each stock item was used last year.
	Find out if any new equipment will be needed next year.
	Will there be any special projects next year like bulk mailings, etc.?
	What nonstock supply items were used this year?
	Will they be used again next year?
	Should they be stocked? (Quantity buying for lower cost)
	Decide format for budget.
	Get prices and extend item costs.

Total budget.

Decide how many copies and for whom.

Project supply needs for next fiscal year.

-/-

Arrange steps in logical order and assign symbols			
	?	1.	How much of each stock item was used last year? (Check requisitions.)
	?	2.	What nonstock supply items were used this year?
	*	3.	Decide if item 2 should be stocked.
	?	4.	Will company letterhead change? (May need to dispose of current letterhead and buy all new.)
	*	5.	Decide how much should be allowed for contingencies for next year.
	!	6.	Project supply needs for next year.
	?	7.	What are current prices on each item in 5?
	!	8.	Extend prices to determine projected costs.
	*	9	Decide if new equipment will be needed and if so, what equipment?
	?	10.	If new equipment is needed, what will it cost?
	!	11.	Total budget.
	*	12.	Decide on format for budget.
	*	13.	Decide how many copies and for whom.
	!	14.	Have budget typed.

-/-

A quick glance at the task chart will reveal what input is needed and indicate that several input steps might be worked on simultaneously by one or more members of the office staff. Similarly, depending on the task, several imperatives could possibly be assigned simultaneously. However, in our example, this would not be possible because each imperative is dependent on the one preceding it. The decisions you will have to make stand out clearly on the task chart. In our example, decisions 5, 9, and 12 could be made at almost any time during the progress of the task, but should be made no later than where they fall on the task chart.

Caution: Don't devote more time to a project than the project is worth. Consider the payoff value of the task in relation to your goal or primary purpose. A high payoff deserves more time (if necessary) than a low payoff. For example, you probably would not devote the same amount of time to a $20,000 per year customer as you would to a $50,000 per year customer.

TIME NORMS

When you or members of your staff have recurring tasks to do, keep track of how much time these tasks normally take. If necessary, break the task down into measurable parts. Figure 3–1 is a suggested form for recording time norms. Such a record will:

1. Point up any task that seems to take a disproportionate amount of time. You may want to reevaluate the wisdom of doing this task.
2. Assist in realistically scheduling work. Any future significant deviation from the task norm will indicate a need for time management action.
3. Give you a record for cost-out purposes. Lawyers and other service people often use such a record as a basis for charges.
4. Help you in establishing a deadline for completion of task. A deadline is your most time-wise friend.

Caution: If the time norm is known to the person doing the task, there is the danger of Parkinson's Law taking over. In other words, the task may expand to fit the time norm. To avoid this, encourage the person to think of the time norm as a record to beat.

PROCRASTINATION DRAWER

Procrastination is a time-consuming habit; but calculated procrastination can save time. Some problems, if left alone, will resolve themselves. Why not keep a desk drawer for such problems?

If a problem in your procrastination drawer becomes urgent, you can always say you've had it under study, pull it out, and go to work on

```
TIME NORMS

┌──────────────────────────────────────────────┬──────────────┐
│              ACTIVITY OR TASK                │  TIME NORM   │
├──────────────────────────────────────────────┼──────────────┤
│                                              │              │
├──────────────────────────────────────────────┼──────────────┤
│                                              │              │
├──────────────────────────────────────────────┼──────────────┤
│                                              │              │
├──────────────────────────────────────────────┼──────────────┤
│                                              │              │
├──────────────────────────────────────────────┼──────────────┤
│                                              │              │
├──────────────────────────────────────────────┼──────────────┤
│                                              │              │
├──────────────────────────────────────────────┼──────────────┤
│                                              │              │
├──────────────────────────────────────────────┼──────────────┤
│                                              │              │
├──────────────────────────────────────────────┼──────────────┤
│                                              │              │
├──────────────────────────────────────────────┼──────────────┤
│                                              │              │
└──────────────────────────────────────────────┴──────────────┘
```

Figure 3–1. Time Norms

it. It's risky but, on the other hand, you may save hours not doing some jobs that will never need to be done anyway.

Keep a Procrastination Record (Figure 3–2) in the front of your procrastination drawer. This will save time when you are looking for an item in the drawer and will be a reminder of when to review or take action on the item.

PROCRASTINATION RECORD			
Item	Date In	Review Date	Future Action

Figure 3–2. Procrastination Record

Caution: Avoid using your procrastination drawer to put off a task that you know you should do.

DELEGATION PLANNING GUIDE

If you have projects with due dates spread over several months, a Planning Guide will keep you on target. See Figure 3–3. It will also reveal to you at a glance the major projects that are in the hopper—vital information you need to schedule your department's work.

DELEGATION PLANNING GUIDE

Instructions:
1. Enter "D" in month task is delegated.
2. Divide projected completion month diagonally.
3. Enter "C" in top triangle of projected completion month.
4. When task is completed, enter "✓" in lower triangle if completed as projected. If not completed as projected, enter "✓" in actual month of completion.

TITLE OF TASK	Delegated to		Month task delegated/completed					
			JAN	FEB	MAR	APR	MAY	JUNE
(sample entries) Equipment Inventory	Bill Jones				D	C / ✓		
Stock Inventory	Fred Smith					D	C /	✓
Budget Report	Mary Brown					D	✓	C /

Figure 3–3. Delegation Planning Guide

RESPONSIBILITY CHART

The Responsibility Chart (Figure 3–4) is a tool to keep you from overlooking someone who should be in on a specific task or problem solving. Leaving out a key person will often result in having to backtrack or start over. It could also result in miscommunication, which is one of the biggest time displacers.

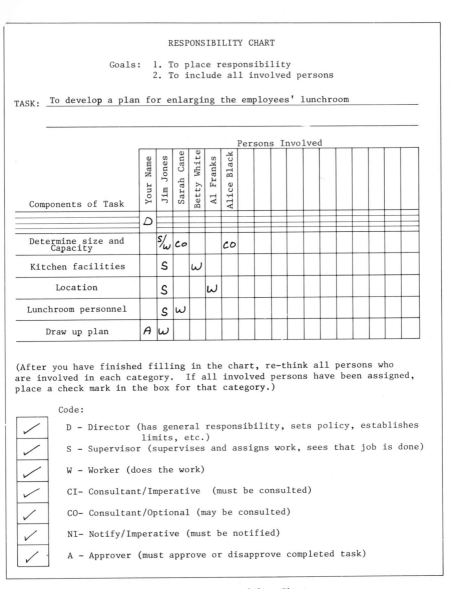

RESPONSIBILITY CHART

Goals: 1. To place responsibility
        2. To include all involved persons

TASK: To develop a plan for enlarging the employees' lunchroom

Components of Task	Your Name	Jim Jones	Sarah Cane	Betty White	Al Franks	Alice Black										
	D															
Determine size and Capacity	S/W	CO			CO											
Kitchen facilities	S		W													
Location	S			W												
Lunchroom personnel	S	W														
Draw up plan	A	W														

Persons Involved

(After you have finished filling in the chart, re-think all persons who
are involved in each category. If all involved persons have been assigned,
place a check mark in the box for that category.)

Code:

✓	D – Director (has general responsibility, sets policy, establishes limits, etc.)
✓	S – Supervisor (supervises and assigns work, sees that job is done)
✓	W – Worker (does the work)
✓	CI– Consultant/Imperative (must be consulted)
✓	CO– Consultant/Optional (may be consulted)
✓	NI– Notify/Imperative (must be notified)
✓	A – Approver (must approve or disapprove completed task)

Figure 3–4. Responsibility Chart

Suppose your company has added employees and the employees' lunchroom is now too small. The company's Board of Directors has decided the lunchroom should be enlarged and has commissioned you to bring them a plan for accomplishing this. So your task is to develop a plan for enlarging the employees' lunchroom.

The first step would be to break the task down into components, such as, determine how big the new lunchroom should be and what its capacity should be, determine what changes are needed in the kitchen facilities, determine whether there is enough room to expand in the present location or if a location should be found elsewhere in the building, determine if number of lunchroom employees should be increased.

List these components on the Responsibility Chart.

Next, list the persons who will be in any way involved in this task. List your own name first and place a D in the square immediately under your name. This will indicate to all concerned that you are the director of the task. Under each person's name, place the appropriate code letter opposite any component of the task that involves that person. The code letters are listed on the lower part of the Responsibility Chart.

In Figure 3–4, we assigned Jim Jones, your administrative assistant, to be supervisor of the task and so we placed an S in all the squares under his name to indicate that he will supervise all components of the task. Jim will also decide on size and capacity, so we put a W as well as an S in his square for that component. Jim will probably need help to do that work (deciding on size and capacity) and so we have given him the option of calling on Sarah Cane in the Personnel Division to advise him on the number of employees using the lunchroom. So we placed CO (consultant/optional) in Sarah's square for that component. Jim also has the option of discussing size and capacity with Alice Black, President of the Employees' Association. And so we placed a CO in Alice's square for that component. We would have placed a CI (consultant/imperative) in Alice's square for that component if we had felt it to be a necessity to include the employees in the plans to enlarge their lunchroom. Then Jim would not have had the option of talking to Alice about size and capacity, he would have had to include her.

As supervisor, Jim will supervise the workers. The director determines who will be the workers in each component, but the supervisor actually assigns the work and sees that it gets done.

Jim will do the last component (draw up the plan) himself after he has received the reports on all the other components from the workers.

You, as director, will approve or disapprove the plan.

After you have filled in the upper portion of the Responsibility Chart, look at each symbol listed in the lower portion of the chart and place a checkmark in the box opposite the symbol if you are satisfied with the assignment you have made in the upper portion of the chart. For example, you were assigned by the Board as the director, so place a checkmark in the box in front of D. (As an executive, you may delegate a task to a subordinate giving him/her the general responsibility for it.

Then that subordinate would be the director of the task and s/he would make up the Responsibility Chart for the task.)

S: Have you assigned a supervisor and are you satisfied with the assignment? If so, place a checkmark in the box in front of S.

W: Have you assigned a worker for each component of the task? If so, place a checkmark in the box in front of W.

CI: Has everyone in your organization who should be consulted about any component of the task been listed? If so, put a checkmark in the box in front of CI.

CO: Has everyone in the organization who would have information, training, or experience that would be beneficial in the execution of any component of the task been listed? If so, put a checkmark in the box in front of CO.

NI: Has everyone who must be notified about the task or any component of it been listed? If so, place a checkmark in the box in front of NI.

A: Has someone been designated to approve or disapprove the completed task? (This would normally be the director, but conceivably it could be someone else. In our example it could have been the Board of Directors.) If the Approver has been designated, place a checkmark in the box in front of A.

After the plan for enlarging the employees' lunchroom has been completed and you have approved it, you would take it to the Board of Directors who had originally requested it. If the Board adopts it and gives you a go-ahead, you would develop a new Responsibility Chart for the task of enlarging the lunchroom according to the adopted plan.

YOUR PROFESSIONAL ASSISTANT

We hesitate to call a person a "tool," but secretaries have been given many labels such as: office secretary, office girl, Girl Friday, and the like. Conversely, many stenographers, telephone operators, file clerks, and account clerks have been misnamed secretary. By whatever names they are called, all of these people are important to the success of any business or profession. It has been our experience that people want to be recognized for the specific contributions they make to their organizations. Most bookkeepers want to be called bookkeepers, most telephone operators want to be called telephone operators, and most secretaries want to be called secretaries.

There are different kinds of secretaries denoting different levels of professionalism, just as there are different levels of management. There is middle management and top management. Usually top management will have executive secretaries, administrative secretaries, or professional assistants. In our seminars we have been aware of all of these titles and others that denote high quality of performance. It seems to us that a secretary who can, together with her chief, be an effective working team regardless of the management level, is a secretary with professional standing and a real asset to her boss and their organization.

So when we speak of your secretary or your assistant throughout this text, we are speaking of a person highly trained in all the facets of office management, human relations, communications, and organization, as well as the skill areas of typing and shorthand. We are speaking of a real professional, your most valuable time management tool. See Chapter 9 for ways this employee can help you in your effective use of time.

YOUR WORK AREA

Time can slip away from you just in your getting started on a task if your work area is not organized. Although individuals vary in their likes and dislikes and in their work habits, the consensus among many successful executives is:

1. Your desk should be cleared of all work except the specific task you are working on. This increases your concentration on the task at hand.
2. Your desk should be organized so that you do not spend time looking for things such as a felt-tip pen, pair of scissors, paper clips, ruler, stapler, staple remover, paper, envelopes, memo pads, and so on. *A place for everything and everything in its place* is a time-wise rule.
3. An adequate work surface is a must. A desk alone is not enough. You need also a work table or counter behind your desk or as an arm to your desk.
4. Your desk should be situated against a wall or partition which you face while working. This will ensure minimum distraction and maximum productivity. Place your desk so that you must turn away from it to give visitors your full attention.
5. Desk-level lighting is more concentrated than overhead lighting. It not only saves on electrical expense, but reduces

noise. People tend to walk slower and talk lower in an area of localized lighting.

6. Your office should be arranged with a working area and a meeting area. Meeting chairs should move easily. See Figure 3–5.

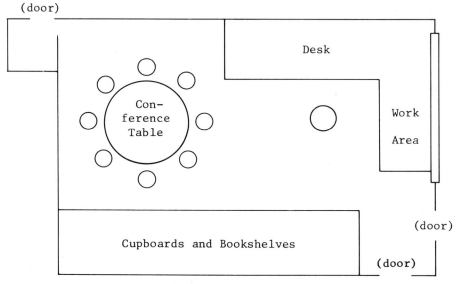

Figure 3–5. Work Area

7. There should be two clocks in your office—one where you can see it clearly and one where your visitors can't escape it.

8. If you travel a lot, a place to change clothes and store a piece of luggage is a time-saver.

When surprised (because of insufficient
planning) an octopus will turn white,
then red, cover its head, and run away.

4

A Time
to Do Paperwork

WHAT TO DO ABOUT ACCUMULATED PAPERWORK

Even if you set your priorities for each day and follow your Daily Organizer (Figure 2–3), there are times when paperwork will pile up on your desk. It is inevitable. Here is a system for wearing down that pile of accumulated tasks.

First, find the time to work on accumulated paperwork. If you can, schedule a day or a half-day for it. You can accomplish much more in a block of time than you can in little bits and pieces of time. If you cannot schedule a block of time, an alternative would be to work one, two, or more paperwork tasks into your Daily Organizer. Make a point of picking out one or two of the highest priority tasks from your accumulated paperwork every day.

When an octopus reacts in panic, it moves backwards and cannot see where it's going.

How To Surmount The Unsurmountable

Assuming that you have found a block of time, either by deliberately scheduling a day or half-day for accumulated paperwork or by working on a Saturday morning, here's how to surmount that "unsurmountable" stack of accumulated tasks.

1. Pick out the most important tasks, as many as you think you can accomplish that day. Add a couple of extra in case you are able to accomplish more than you thought you would.
2. List each task you have picked out on a separate slip of paper or a 3 x 5 card.
3. Lay the cards on your desk and move them around until you have them in the order in which you will do them. When doing this:
   a. Intersperse dull, monotonous tasks with more interesting ones.
   b. Intersperse active (physical) tasks with passive (mental) tasks.
   c. As much as possible, group similar tasks into one, such as all phone calls, all letters to dictate, and so forth.
4. Now pick up the slips in the proper order, with the first task on top.
5. Place the stack on a corner of your desk where it is visible to you but out of the way of your work area.
6. When you have completed the first task, turn that slip over, starting a pile of completed tasks. Have only one job visible at a time—the one you are working on. This will help you to concentrate on the task you are doing.

7. If you have a task that will take a great deal of time, such as a report to write, divide it into segments and make a separate slip for each segment. Scatter the segments throughout your pile of tasks to do. This will keep you from getting bored with the long, drawn-out task, and will allow you to complete some other smaller jobs and give you a feeling of accomplishment in the meantime.

How To Keep Paperwork from Accumulating

How do you keep stacks of paperwork from accumulating? There are few executives who do not have a backlog of paperwork to do; but there are habits you can develop to help you keep your paperwork from getting completely out of hand.

Never handle a piece of paper more than once.   Every time you pick up a piece of paper, whether it is a letter, a report, a phone message, do something with it other than putting it in a "to do" pile. If it is a letter that requires your reply, answer it *now*. If it is a report that you need to read and digest, do it *now*. If you don't have time to read and digest it now, delegate the task to someone else who will be able to pick out the highlights and give you a brief summary. The main thing is to get the report off your desk *now*.

R. Alec Mackenzie, in an interview reported in *U.S. News & World Report*, was asked:

Question: Most people in business and the professions complain about a tide of time-consuming paperwork. How does an individual keep from being swamped?

Answer: The first rule is to delegate as much work as you can to others. If you don't delegate, the paper will come to you. The most common cause of paperwork frustration is indecision. The average manager should be able to make an immediate decision on about 80 percent of the items in his "in" box. Typically, he won't know a bit more about the subject tomorrow, or several days from now. The person who gets accustomed to making decisions right off the bat will find that they are as good as though he had put the issues aside for two or three days to think about them. And then he has to reread them to recall what they are about.

Two benefits arise from quick decisions. One is that you gain time—and in a competitive situation, time is critical. Second, you have more time to correct the occasional decision that was wrong. As you postpone a decision, you get to a point of irreversibility. When you finally make it, it's too late to change—and the risk of being wrong is enhanced.[1]

[1]From a copyrighted interview in *U.S. News & World Report*, December 3, 1973.

Train your professional assistant not to bring you every piece of paper that comes into the office.   Make your assistant responsible for routing mail to your support people, answering routine mail, discarding mail of no use such as advertisements that are of no interest to you, filing mail containing information that needs to be kept but that you don't need to see now.

Work out a sorting system with your professional assistant for mail that you need to see.   One technique would be to have a folder marked *urgent* for mail that needs your attention today; another folder marked *important but not urgent;* and another marked *information only.* You may want to use a different colored folder for each category.

Have your secretary read letters, reports, periodicals, and so forth, and underscore the main points.   Say a lengthy letter comes addressed to you. Your assistant opens and reads it, noting that a request is made and a deadline for reply is given. The letter is of a nature that your assistant cannot answer it for you; however, s/he can attach pertinent information s/he knows you will need to answer the letter; s/he underlines the exact request that is made and draws a red arrow or circles the deadline date. Now when you pick up the letter you see at a glance what is needed, you have the information available, and, while still holding the letter, you turn to your dictating machine and dictate the answer, placing the letter in the dictation folder for your assistant. Thus you have taken care of a piece of paperwork that you might otherwise have added to your accumulation of paperwork until you had time to read the lengthy letter again and look up the information to reply to it.

Cut down on mass copying and routing of magazine articles.   If an article is routed, have your assistant underline the key points so that those receiving it can skim it quickly.

Make marginal notes on incoming mail.   Your professional assistant can then reply for you.

Reply by phone rather than by mail.   Using the phone may take less time.

Have your name removed from mailing lists, if you receive a lot of "junk" mail.   Write to:

Mail Preference Service
Direct Mail Marketing
6 East 43rd Street
New York, N.Y. 10017

Ask your colleagues not to send you "for your information" copies of letters and report if you can do without them.   It is often not essential for you to see such material.

✓ **Insist that a recommendation be submitted along with any problem statement that comes to you.**   This will assure you that the person who has the problem has given some thought to solving it and is not merely passing the buck to you. Sometimes all you will have to do is approve the recommendation if it seems logical to you.

Require that reports of more than three pages carry a cover page.   A cover page with the subject of the report, the date it was prepared, and the name of the reporter will save you the time you would otherwise spend looking through the report to find this information. It will also save filing time if the report is to be filed.

If possible, form the habit of processing routine paperwork at the same time every day.   It will become a habit and you will not be likely to procrastinate your paperwork. Also, others will become aware that this is the time of day when you are not apt to be available to them.

Remember: A place for everything and everything in its place.   This old adage can spare you much wasted time.

Make a periodic check on reports you prepare.   Follow each report through to its final destination.

- ▶ Who really reads it?
- ▶ Who uses it?
- ▶ Is the same information being compiled in another department?

You may find a report that is only glanced at, passed on, and eventually filed or destroyed. That one could be eliminated from your stack of paperwork as it is obviously no longer needed.

or

On an office bulletin board, post samples of all reports your company or your department prepares. Ask the company executives to review each one and sign or initial only those that should be continued. The same could be done with office forms. There may be several that are obsolete.

or

Another way to cut down on the number of reports being prepared is to cost out reports and bill each department that prepares a new report or requests a copy of an existing one.

Take a critical look at your correspondence, especially intra-organizational letters and memorandums.

1. Is time being spent dictating, transcribing, and delivering intra-office mail when:

   ▶ a phone call would suffice?
   ▶ a handwritten note would be enough?
   ▶ a printed routing slip or attachment memo could be used? See Figures 6–2 and 6–3.

2. Does your correspondence contain complete information the first time, thereby eliminating a whole file of letters back and forth in order to accomplish what one letter should have accomplished in the first place? Chapter 6 contains help on letter writing.

Save time on once-in-a-while tasks by cataloging pertinent information that you can use the next time you do the task. Such information as person to contact, phone number, prices, schedules, travel arrangements, and so forth can be recorded in this manner. This will cut down on repetitive detail work.

Use a mail summary. Have your secretary record each day's mail on the Mail Summary (see Figure 4–1). Train your assistant to use judgment in what to record; not every piece of mail need be listed. Do not record mail that requires no action. The purpose of the Mail Summary is not to have a complete list of mail received, but to keep track of important mail until necessary action has been completed. Figure 4–1 shows how the Mail Summary would look when you receive it from your secretary.

The first item indicates that your assistant routed a letter from Jones, dated October 4, requesting a sales summary by November 15, to Sam Peterson (your Sales Manager).

The second item shows that your assistant replied to an inquiry letter concerning your organization's refund policy, which is Policy No. 489.

The third item lists a request for you to accept nomination for president-elect of your service club.

When you look over the Mail Summary, you note the first item and decide you want to see a copy of the sales summary Sam sends to Jones. So you put "see copy" in the column for special instructions. If you had wanted to see the original summary before it was mailed to Jones, you would have put "see original."

You return the Mail Summary to your professional assistant. Your

	MAIL SUMMARY FOR

Oct 4, 1978

Item Dated	From	Subject/Action	Action Due	Disposition	Spec. Instr.	Act. Complete Date	By
10/4	Jones	Reg Sales Sum.	11/15	to Sam Petersen			
10/2	Smith	Inquiry re- referral pol.	—	Replied Pol. # 489		10/4	
10/3	Whitley	Nom. for Pres. Elect	10/10	attached			

Figure 4–1. Mail Summary

assistant notes any special instructions you have added and passes them along. In our example, s/he would contact Sam Peterson and ask him to forward a copy of the sales summary when he has it finished.

When Sam Peterson notifies your assistant that the job is done, your assistant enters the date the action was completed, along with Sam Peterson's initials, and also gives you the copy of the sales summary you requested.

Your professional assistant keeps the Mail Summaries chronologically in a loose-leaf binder and checks every day to see that action due dates are being met.

Before designing any new form, consider:

1. Is it necessary? What will it accomplish? Can the procedure it is designed for be simplified or eliminated?
2. Is there a form already in use that could be modified to include this information or procedure?
3. What effect will the new form have on other departments? Will it make their work easier? Increase their work? Have no effect?
4. How much money and time will it cost to process this form? Consider clerical work, equipment needed, storage of blank forms, filing, handling costs.
5. How much training time in the use of the form will be required?

Design office forms for speed. Office forms should be attractive and functional. Observance of the following suggestions will ensure that the forms are used properly and will thus eliminate the necessity to redo, go back for more information, or prepare additional copies for routing—all of which adds to paperwork and time displacement.

1. All instructions should be printed on the form itself, including number of copies and distribution of copies.
2. Every form should have a title and form number for easy identification. Form numbers should consistently be in the same location on all forms. The lower left-hand corner seems to be the most common place for this information. Also, identify the date of adoption of the form and any date of revision, so the user of the form knows whether the most current form is being used.
3. If completed forms are to be bound, allow enough space for binding.
4. Identify the form by function or department. For example, an application for employment could be assigned No. P-38. The P would denote "Personnel Office" and all personnel office forms would have a P before the form number.
5. When possible, use check lists so that the person filling in the form can place a check mark in the appropriate blank instead of writing out an answer. The less work the form requires, the less time it will displace.

6. If the form is to be filled in on a typewriter, be sure enough space for pica type is allowed. Be sure to allow adequate space for handwritten answers if that is what will be required. Better too much than not enough space.

7. As many office forms as possible should be the same size. Uniform size saves time because it facilitates filing.

8. Consider using treated paper instead of carbons. It is cleaner and faster.

9. Consider whether a form should be padded or loose, continuous strip, fanfold, marginal punched, with or without a stub to be torn off.

10. When you design or redesign a form, consider consulting the people who will be using it. Their suggestions will help make the form workable.

11. Destroy your supply of an obsolete form as soon as the new form has replaced it.

SORTING SYSTEMS TO CONTROL TIME

You need a sorting system for keeping abreast of all your various paperwork tasks. There are probably as many kinds of sorting systems as there are executives. A good sorting system is one that works for you. It may or may not work for your neighbor across the hall. Experiment with sorting systems until you find the one that best suits your needs and saves your time. Then adjust it until you are comfortable with it. It should be flexible enough for you to make minor changes in it as your needs change. Here are some that have been used by executives from middle management up.

3 by 5 Card System

For sorting out accumulated paperwork we recommend the 3 x 5 card system mentioned at the beginning of this chapter under the heading "How to Surmount the Unsurmountable."

Advantage: You see your stack of accumulated paperwork dwindle.

Task Folders

Many executives keep track of current projects by having them laid out in task folders on the counter or bookcase behind their desk. Label each folder across the top with an identifying task/project name and due date, using print large enough to see without picking up the folder. You may want to use a color code to designate different kinds of tasks. Keep all material you need for working on a project in the folder for that specific project.

Advantages: (a) Gets tasks you are not working on off your desk working area, so you can concentrate fully on the one task you *are* working on at any given time. (b) Keeps all papers relating to a specific task together. You do not have to go to the files to dig out what you need before you begin working on a task. Instruct your assistant to put any new material on those tasks in the appropriate task folder instead of with the rest of the incoming mail (unless, of course, it is something that needs your immediate attention).

Next Step Slip

Keep a pad of Next Step Slips (Figure 4–2) on your counter for tasks too big to complete in one sitting. Before you leave a task that is to be continued, fill out the next Step Slip and put it into the task folder.

Advantages: (a) The next time you pick up this task to work on, you know exactly where you left off and no time is wasted reviewing what you have already done. If possible, leave off at a point where the next step is an easy one. This will give you a running start when you return to the project. When the next step is a difficult one, it is easy to procrastinate. (b) When the task is completed, you have a record of the dates you worked on it and how much time it took to complete the task. This may be valuable scheduling information if you have a similar task to do at a later date. Keep these Next Step Slips in a Task Time Displacement binder for easy reference.

Card File Follow-up Organizer

Build a 3 by 5 card-file follow-up organizer to hang on the wall over your desk or counter. The organizer is constructed with slots that will hold the cards. It can be made out of ¼-inch plywood or any lightweight

```
┌─────────────────────────────────────────────────────────────────┐
│                          NEXT STEP                              │
│  The next step is:  _____  │
│  The next step is:  _____  │
│  The next step is:  _____  │
│  The next step is:  _____  │
│  The next step is:  _____  │
│  The next step is:  _____  │
│  The next step is:  _____  │
│  The next step is:  _____  │
│                                                                 │
│                      Time Displacement                          │
│                    (in hours and minutes)                       │
│  Date: _____   Time: _____    │
│  Date: _____   Time: _____    │
│  Date: _____   Time: _____    │
│  Date: _____   Time: _____    │
│  Date: _____   Time: _____    │
│  Date: _____   Time: _____    │
│  Date: _____   Time: _____    │
│  Date: _____   Time: _____    │
│                      TOTAL TIME:                                │
│  TASK/PROJECT: _____ │
│  Due Date: _____  Actual Completion Date: _____  │
└─────────────────────────────────────────────────────────────────┘
```

Figure 4–2. Next Step Slip

material such as fiberboard. Each slot is 2 inches high, 3½ inches wide, and 4½ inches deep, and the organizer is seven slots high and seven slots wide. Label the slots as follows:

▶ The left-hand column of slots is for the current week and is labeled from top to bottom with the days of the week.

▶ The next four vertical rows of slots, except for the bottom slot in each row, are for half-month periods, starting with January 1–15, for a calendar year.

▶ The bottom horizontal row of four slots under the calendar year slots are labeled from left to right: 4th Quarter, 3rd Quarter, 2nd Quarter, and 1st Quarter. Use these slots for items that come up quarterly. At the beginning of each quarter take the items for that quarter and transfer them to the half-month slot when you want them to come to your attention.

▶ Label the three right-hand columns in whatever way best suits your needs. You may want to use these slots for thoughts that occur to you concerning present or future projects, or for ideas that you can use to bring you closer to your goals. You could have a slot for each main goal area of your life, such as, spiritual, mental, physical, financial, business, family, social.

Always carry a supply of 3 by 5 cards with you. At home have a few in each room, the kitchen, living room, den, bedroom, bathroom. Whenever you think of anything you want to remember—a phone call to make, a letter to write, a creative idea, an anniversary or birthday—jot it down on a card. When you get back to your desk, file the card in the appropriate slot.

Advantage: Eliminates searching for notes scribbled on backs of envelopes, on bits of paper torn from a newspaper, or on the back of supermarket tapes. It eliminates rewriting these scribbled notes more legibly, finding a place to put them, and then remembering where you put them. In other words, the system is a practical memory jogger for the fleeting, creative thoughts that come when you are not ready to act on them. It is an organized way to record them, file them, and rethink them at the right time and in the right setting.

Letter-Size Follow-up Organizer

You may prefer a letter-size follow-up organizer. Build it as you would the card-file organizer, but make the slots large enough to take 8½ by 11 paper. Using the right-hand columns for tasks or projects would eliminate having the task folders on your counter. The columns on the left side of the organizer could be a bring-up file, eliminating the need for a tickler file in your desk drawer. (For Tickler File, see next section.)

Tickler File

Your professional assistant may be keeping a Tickler File for you. If not, here is how to set one up.

1. Label one folder for each month of the year and label 31 other folders from 1 to 31. Now you have 43 folders. One more is needed. Label it *Future Years*.

2. Arrange the folders in your desk drawer with the daily (numbered) folders first, then the monthly folders, and last the *Future Years* folder.

Here's how it works:

Suppose it is the morning of June 30. The folder in front is labeled *30*. Take out the things in that folder and lay them on your desk for attention today. Put the *30* folder behind the other numbered folders. Now the front folder is labeled *31*, but it is turned backwards because there are only 30 days in June. Place folder *31* behind the *30* folder, facing front because there are 31 days in July.

Behind the numbered (daily) folders are the monthly folders. The first one this morning is *July*. Since this is the last day of June, take out the *July* folder and distribute the material that is in it into the daily folders. Suppose there is a memo that will need your attention on July 20. Place it in the *20* folder. Then put the *July* folder behind the other monthly folders.

Check the *Future Years* folder during December and distribute items for the next calendar year into the monthly folders.

Advantage: You have an automatic reminder or memory tickler each morning concerning tasks that need your attention. Important items are not forgotten and you save time by not having to search for them.

Office Files

The office files are a sorting system that can get out of hand if not given a critical look annually. One executive we know declares a "Tear Up—Throw Away" day every spring. Each staff member wears old clothes that day and comes prepared to go through the files with a critical eye. Every piece of "dead" paper is torn up and thrown away. A records retention policy should, of course, be established first so that important documents are not tossed out prior to the time for which they legally must be retained. These can be removed and placed in storage for the legal duration.

Advantage: Less bulky files make for faster filing and finding.

HOW TO KEEP YOUR ACUMEN LEVEL HIGH

If your paperwork contains much reading and studying material, you need a high acumen level. Webster defines *acumen* as quickness of perception; penetration; insight. Here are some helps for reading fast, comprehending and retaining what you read, being able to learn new information quickly, and being able to recall it when you need it.

Speedy Reading

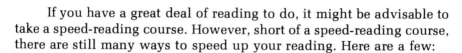

If you have a great deal of reading to do, it might be advisable to take a speed-reading course. However, short of a speed-reading course, there are still many ways to speed up your reading. Here are a few:

1. Practice reading fast. Consciously push yourself. Resist the temptation to go back and reread a word or phrase. Often, the faster you read the more you will comprehend and retain, because your mind does not have time to wander from the train of thought on the printed page. The speed with which you can understand and retain material depends, of course, on the kind of material it is. Highly technical material would have to be read more slowly to be grasped.
2. Be choosy about what you read. When you pick up a periodical, first glance at the table of contents. If there is nothing there that interests you or that will give you information you need to achieve a goal, set it aside.
3. Do the same with books. Look at chapter headings and read only those chapters that will benefit you.
4. When you read articles or book chapters, skim. Read the first paragraph of the article, the first sentence of each paragraph, and the last paragraph. Read complete paragraphs only when the first sentence indicates to you that the paragraph contains information that interests you.
5. Continually build your vocabulary so that fewer unfamiliar words will slow your reading.

Retaining New Information

New information can be retained longer if you observe the following:

1. Do not attempt to cram too much into your mind at one time. Suppose you want to learn a new procedure for doing something. First read over the entire procedure quickly and get an overall picture of what has to be done and what the desired result is. Don't try to remember it in detail at this point. Now go back to the beginning, take the first one or two steps, and fix them clearly in your mind. After steps 1 and 2 are firmly established in your mind, review steps 1 and 2 and learn step 3. Then review steps 1, 2, and 3 and learn step 4. Always go back to the beginning to reinforce what you have already learned.

2. Learn to pace yourself. Intersperse short study periods with activity that does not require as much concentration, or with a complete change of thought.

3. Review often.

4. Use what you learn as soon as possible after learning it.

5. Make your own outline of material that is not already sectioned and proceed to learn it point by point (as in number 1 above).

6. Catalog information you will need but won't need often enough to commit to memory. Do this by setting up a reference file by subject. File copies of articles and notes concerning reference books you have read. Record the title of book, author, publisher, and page number on which the reference appears. If it is a library book, record the library reference number so you can quickly find the book again when you need it. See Figure 4–3.

7. As you do research for a report, record the facts you find and file them in your reference file. You may need them again for another report or speech. In other words, build your own research file. You have to record facts somewhere; it might as well be in a permanent file.

```
                              REFERENCE


Subject: _____

Reference quote:

















Source:   Publication _____   Page No. _____

          Author _____

          Publisher _____

                    _____   Library Reference

                    _____   No.: _____
```

Figure 4–3. Reference (Information)

5

A Time
to Decide

Decision making is the most essential task an executive performs. The act of deciding permeates nearly everything an executive does. Hundreds of minor, spontaneous decisions are effectively made by executives every day, and such decisions are based on knowledge and experience. At the other end of the decision-making scale are the conceptual decisions that grow out of vision. These are the decisions that establish long-range goals, define projects, establish new organizational direction, and bring about change. In between these two extremes are the perplexing managerial problems executives are expected to solve magically. But, as every executive knows, there is no magic to wise decision making.

Decision making is actually a part of problem solving. There would be no decision to make if there were no problem to solve. Problem

To avoid making a decision sometimes an octopus will disappear into the first available crevice.

solving consists of three operations: problem analysis, decision making, and action. Thus, decision making is that part of problem solving that follows study of the problem and is followed by action to carry out the decision.

PROBLEM ANALYSIS

Managerial problems fall into three general areas: 1) deviation from what has happened to what is happening, 2) choosing between alternatives, and 3) deciding rank order.

Analyzing and Solving Deviation Problems

Dale Carnegie says answering the following questions can reduce your worries by 50 percent:[1]

1. What is the problem?
2. What is the cause of the problem?
3. What are all possible solutions to the problem?
4. What is the best solution?

Answering these questions will also reduce by at least 50 percent the time it takes to analyze a problem and arrive at a decision.

What is the problem? This may seem to be too elementary a question to take time to answer. But, unless you can state the problem in

---

[1]Dale Carnegie, *How to Stop Worrying and Start Living* (New York: Simon and Schuster, 1948), p. 40.

three or four typewritten lines, you either don't know what the problem is, or you are trying to deal with several problems at once.

Use the Problem Analysis form, Figure 5–1, to determine the characteristics of the deviation problem.

PROBLEM ANALYSIS

The problem is __brochures and catalogs coming from our printing__

__department are not up to their usual quality standard.__

_____

_____

What is	What is not	Distinction
The paper is 16 lb.	The paper is not 20 lb.	X
The type is light.	The type is not distinct.	X
Printer X did the work.	No one else did the work.	
Work was done on multilith.	Work was not done on any other duplicator.	
Brand S ink was used.	No other brand ink was used.	
All brochures and catalogs in last run are affected.	Brochures and catalogs in previous runs are not affected.	X

Figure 5–1. Problem Analysis

1. Finish the sentence, "The problem is . . ." in as few words as you can. For example, suppose you are the top executive of a company that sells small appliances. Your sales manager has brought to your attention the fact that the advertising materials are not up to the quality that they have been and he predicts sales will be lost because of inferior PR materials. You can state the problem this way: "The problem is brochures and catalogs coming from our printing department are not up to their usual quality standard."
2. In the column "What is," list all the characteristics of the brochures and catalogs that you can think of. For example, "The paper is 16 pound."
3. In the column "What is not," list the converse statements to the statements of "What is."
4. Wherever a distinction exists, place a check in the column "Distinction."

Analyzing deviation problems in this way will very quickly make apparent the distinctions between what is and what is not. A study of these distinctions will direct you to the cause(s) of the problem.

What is the cause of the problem?   Use the Problem Cause Analysis form, Figure 5–2, to get at the cause of the problem.

1. From the Problem Analysis form, carry over the distinctions you noted to the "Distinction" column on the Problem Cause Analysis form.
2. For each distinction, list the possible cause.
3. For each possible cause, determine the "Why" or "Why's" by asking questions of the people involved.

We have used a simple example to point out how the process of Problem Analysis and Problem Cause Analysis works. This process saves top executives many hours in analyzing complex deviation problems.

What are all possible solutions to the problem?   Most problems faced by executives have alternative solutions. Peter Drucker says:

A decision without an alternative is a desperate gambler's throw, no matter how carefully thought through it might be. . . . If one has thought through alternatives during the decision-making process, one has something to fall

PROBLEM CAUSE ANALYSIS

(Use in conjunction with Problem Analysis form)

Distinction	Possible Cause	Why	Why
Paper is 16 lb.	Printer did not have enough 20 lb. paper in stock for last run.	1. Purchasing Dept. ordered 16 lb. instead of 20 lb. 2. Printer did not use good judgment.	Stock clerk made error on last inventory.
Type is light.	Inferior paper used – see above		
All brochures and catalogs in last run are affected.	Inferior paper used on last run.	See above	See above

Figure 5–2. Problem Cause Analysis

back on, something that has already been thought through, that has been studied, that is understood. Without such an alternative, one is likely to flounder dismally when reality proves a decision to be inoperative.[2]

Problem analysis at the executive level is seldom done by one person. It is most often done by a group of people often with opposing

[2]Peter F. Drucker, *The Executive* (New York: Harper & Row, Publishers, Inc., 1966), p. 150. Copyright © 1966, 1967 by Peter F. Drucker. By permission of the publisher.

viewpoints. Time-wise executives use opposition to think through alternatives. They use conflict of opinion as a tool to look at all major aspects of important problems.

Use the Problem Solution Analysis form to list alternative solutions. See Figure 5–3.

PROBLEM SOLUTION ANALYSIS

Problem Cause #1: __Stock clerk error__

Alternate Solution #1: __If first time error has occurred, point out__ error and the chain reaction it had to the stock clerk.

Alternate Solution #2: __Hold more frequent evaluation of work of__ stock clerk.

Alternate Solution #3: __Conduct in-house seminar aimed at increasing__ pride in work for all employees.

Problem Cause #2: __Printer's judgment__

Alternate Solution #1: __Give printer latitude to question the use of__ stock on hand if it appears to be inferior.

Alternate Solution #2: __Hold more frequent evaluation of work of__ printer.

Alternate Solution #3: __Same as Alternate #3 under Cause #1.__

Figure 5–3. Problem Solution Analysis

1. Determine the cause(s) of the problem and enter them on the "Cause" line. If you have used the Problem Cause Analysis form, this information is at your fingertips.
2. Depending on the magnitude of the problem, list two, three, four, or more possible alternative solutions to the problem—as many as you can think of, but at least two.

What is the best solution?   See the next section, "Solving Alternative Problems."

Analyzing and Solving Alternative Problems

You can combine judgment and mathematics to determine the best possible solution to any alternative problem. For example, suppose you are a Sales Manager; your professional assistant has been promoted and you need to find a replacement for her/him. Use the "Best Possible Solution Matrix" (Figure 5–4) to choose a replacement from among the top applicants for the position.[3]

1. Under "Requirements" list all the essential qualifications for the position—the qualifications in your professional assistant that you cannot do without.
2. Under "Preferences" list the qualifications that you would like your professional assistant to have but that are not absolutely essential. Weight these in the "Weight" column on a scale of from 1 to 10, 10 being the most preferred and 1 being least preferred.
3. Now take the three top applicants and fill in their required qualifications. For example, Applicant A has a B.A. in Business Administration, has four years' experience as a secretary, takes shorthand at 120 words per minute, and types at 60 words per minute.
4. Fill in their preferred but nonessential qualifications. For example, Applicant A has had four years' experience with your agency, has had no experience in sales, and does have writing talent.
5. For the first preference listed, take the applicant who has the most of that preference and write a circled 10 in the square for that applicant and that preference. Rate all other applicants for

---

[3]The *Best Possible Solution Matrix* is an adaptation of Charles Rice's *House Decision Matrix*. Charles Rice is President of IMPOD, Inc., and part-time faculty member of University of Colorado's College of Business and Administration.

BEST POSSIBLE SOLUTION MATRIX

Requirements		App. A	App. B	App. C	
BA in Bus. Adm.		BA	BA+16	MA	
3 yrs. experience as secretary		4 yrs.	5 yrs.	3 yrs.	
Shorthand 125 Typing 70		120 60	125 70	125 60	
Preferences	Wt.	A	B	C	
In-house experience	5	4 yrs. (10) 50	2 yrs. (5) 25	1 yr. (2) 10	
Sales Experience	5	0 yrs (0) 0	3 yrs. (6) 30	5 yrs. (10) 50	
Sp. talent in P.R. Writing	7	yes (10) 70	no (0) 0	yes (10) 70	
Total Preference:		120	55	130	

Negative Factors:

App. A. Typing speed — 10 ⎫
Shorthand speed — 5 ⎬ 9
May not keep up with work ⎭ $\times$ 2
$\frac{9}{2} \times 2 = \times 2$

App. C. Overqualified with M.A. — — $\frac{9 \ 10}{7} = \times 70$
May not be satisfied, and leave as soon as she finds position to match qualifications.

Figure 5–4. Best Possible Solution Matrix

that desirable qualification down from 10. For example, applicant A has had four years' experience with your agency; applicant B has worked two years for your agency; and applicant C has worked one year for your agency. Therefore, assign a ⑩ to applicant A, a ⑤ to applicant B, and a ② to applicant C, for preference In-house experience. Follow this same procedure for each preference.

6. Multiply the weight for each preference by each applicant's circled figure and enter the product in red in the appropriate square. For example, applicant A has a ⑩ for preference *In-house Experience* and *In-house Experience* is weighted 5. Therefore, multiply ⑩ by 5 to arrive at 50. Write 50 in red. Follow this procedure for each preference and each applicant.

7. Add the red figures for each applicant to find their Total Preference Score.

8. Search for negative factors. In our example it looks mathematically as though applicant C is the best qualified applicant. However, you now use your judgment to determine what negative factors are present and their seriousness.

9. List negative factors for each of the two best alternates. In our example, you may consider applicant C to be too highly qualified for the position due to the M.A. degree. If so, you would list it as a negative factor.

10. For each negative factor, assign an "importance" weight from a scale of 1 to 10—10 being most important and 1 being only slightly important.

11. Assign a "likelihood" weight from a scale of 1 to 10—10 being that the likelihood will undoubtedly occur, and 1 being that it is not likely to happen.

12. Multiply the importance by the likelihood to determine the Warning Score.

13. Do not relate the Warning Score mathematically to the Preference Score. Use it as a guide to help you make a balanced decision.

Analyzing and Solving Rank-Order Problems

The Decision Matrix, developed by George L. Morrisey, can be used to solve rank-order problems in the least possible time.[4] See Figure 5–5.

Suppose you are the marketing executive for a large quick-service food establishment. Your firm is headquartered in New York City and you have sold franchises in cities throughout the Eastern states. Your firm now wants to expand to other cities across the United States. Your task is to determine the rank order of cities in which your firm will offer franchises. You have a list of preferred cities and you have already gathered information concerning markets, population, federal and state government regulations, and so forth, applying to each proposed location.

[4]George L. Morrisey, MOR Associates, Buena Park, Calif., 1974.

DECISION MATRIX	1 Detroit	2 Chicago	3 Indianapolis	4 Miami	5 Dallas	6 St. Paul	7 Phoenix	8 San Francisco	9 San Diego	10 Portland	11 Seattle	12 Honolulu	TOTAL X
1 Detroit				X		X				X	X		4 1
2 Chicago				X		X				X	X		4 2
3 Indianapolis				X	X	X				X	X		5 3
4 Miami						X		X	X			X	4 4
5 Dallas						X				X		X	3 5
6 St. Paul											X		1 6
7 Phoenix								X	X	X	X		4 7
8 San Francisco										X	X		2 8
9 San Diego										X	X	X	3 9
10 Portland													0 10
11 Seattle													0 11
12 Honolulu													0 12
	1	2	3	4	5	6	7	8	9	10	11	12	
VERTICAL (spaces)	0	1	2	0	3	0	6	5	6	2	3	8	
HORIZONTAL (X's)	4	4	5	4	3	1	4	2	3	0	0	0	
GRAND TOTAL	4	5	7	4	6	1	10	7	9	2	3	8	
RANK ORDER	7	6	4	7	5	10	1	4	2	9	8	3	

Figure 5–5. Decision Matrix*

1. On the Decision Matrix, list each city twice: once on a horizontal line and again on the corresponding vertical line.
2. Evaluate city No. 1 against city No. 2. If city No. 1 is better than city No. 2, place an X in the box on the line with city No. 1, under city No. 2. If city No. 1 is less desirable than city No. 2, leave the space blank on that line under No. 2. Repeat with each remain-

*Courtesy George L. Morrisey, MOR ASSOCIATES, Buena Park, California, 1974.

ing city on that line. For example, compare Detroit with Chicago, then Detroit with Indianapolis, and so forth.

3. Now go down to city No. 2 and compare it with all the remaining cities. Repeat for each city on the list.

4. Total the X's across for each number and enter in "Horizontal" box at bottom of the page. Total the blank spaces down for each number and enter in "Vertical" box at bottom of page. Add the numbers for the totals.

5. The city with the largest total will be No. 1 in rank order.

6. If two or more alternatives have the same total (in our example Detroit, Miami, and Seattle have; and Indianapolis, San Francisco, and Honolulu have), reevaluate them against each other to determine their rank order.

TAKING ACTION

The key to making effective decisions quickly lies in knowing the kind of problem that is demanding attention (deviation, alternative, or rank order) and the kind of action that is needed. Action may be needed even before the final decision is made. There are four kinds of action an executive can take:

Interim Action: Taken when cause of problem cannot be located or corrective action is not feasible.

Corrective Action: Taken to eliminate the cause that produced the problem.

Preventive Action: Taken to change a situation that may cause a problem.

Contingency Action: Taken only if first plan of action fails. Where the stakes are high, an alternative action should be decided upon. It is a standby action to be taken if need be. For example, if the main speaker at a large convention fails to show up and you have chosen a standby speaker, you have taken contingency action.

MAKING DECISIONS WORK

The best decision is of no use unless it works. It will work only if the people involved have a mind to make it work. Here are some ways you can presell your decision to those who will be affected by it.

1. When decisions will affect others, involve them in the decision-making process as much as possible. You will arrive at better decisions in less time.
2. Make sure those affected know why the decision was made. They will accept it more readily if they know the reason for it.
3. Make sure those affected know that you are aware they are affected. Most people want to be recognized. If you don't show them that you know how your decision is going to affect them, they will find ways to tell you how it affects them. These could be time-consuming ways—anything from slacking off to a work stoppage.
4. Present a decision on a "try out" basis. A change is always easier to adjust to if it's not written in stone for all time.
5. Invite constructive comments on how it's working. Those affected will usually feel responsible for helping to make it work.
6. Tell those affected how it will benefit them. They will cooperate more readily.

Drucker reminds us:

Decisions are made by men. Men are fallible; at their best their works do not last long. Even the best decision has a high probability of being wrong. Even the most effective one eventually becomes obsolete.[5]

TIME-WISE CRISIS MANAGEMENT

The best way to manage a crisis is, of course, to avoid having it. What happens today is ideally the result of plans made a week, a month, or a year ago. But, as Robert Burns put it, "The best laid schemes of mice and men gang aft a-gley." Crises are very real, usually time-consuming, and often unavoidable.

Nevertheless, a crisis situation can result in time benefits for you. Here's how:

1. When you are faced with a crisis demanding an immediate decision, do not hedge or compromise. Drucker says:

   The surgeon who only takes out half the tonsils or half the appendix risks as much infection or shock as if he did the whole job. And he has not cured the condition, has indeed made it worse. He either operates

[5]Drucker, *Effective Executive*, p. 139.

or he doesn't. Similarly, the effective decision maker either acts or he doesn't act. He does not take half action.[6]

It may be necessary to make an interim or stopgap decision in a crisis situation; but as soon as the emergency is over, arrive at a final decision that covers all bases.

2. Remember, you can't see the picture when you are in the frame. After the crisis is past, stand back from it and view it with a critical eye.

   ▶ What caused the crisis? Could you take steps now to avoid a similar crisis occurring again?

   ▶ Knowing what you know now, what did you do during the crisis that you would not repeat? Why would you not repeat it? What alternative action could you have taken?

   ▶ What did you do during the crisis that was innovative and effective? Can you use this innovative action to reap time rewards in other areas?

   ▶ Did the crisis point up particular strengths in staff members that you can use to solve time problems in the future?

3. Have faith in your resources to meet great emergencies and crises. Most people use only a small percentage of their strength and ability until some crisis occurs. In retrospect, they usually are surprised by how well they handled the situation. Approach every business emergency or crisis with determination to emerge on top of it and you will see how much greater your executive resources are than you had supposed.

DEVICES FOR CREATING IDEAS

Brainstorming.   Brainstorming is a method for getting a great many ideas from a group of people for later evaluation. Every idea, no matter how far out, is recorded without criticism. A participant may also add onto an idea already presented by someone else. After a set period of time for generating ideas has elapsed, the group evaluates the ideas presented.

Solo Brainstorming.   This is the same as brainstorming but done by one person. When you are faced with a knotty problem and need some fresh ideas to solve it, think about it for five or ten minutes just before you

<hr>

[6]Drucker, *Effective Executive*, p. 157.

fall asleep at night. The next morning have a solo-brainstorming session while dressing. Usually ideas will pop into your consciousness from your subconscious mind.

Moonlighting. If you awaken in the night and ideas are tumbling over each other in your mind, resist the urge to pull up the covers and go back to sleep. Instead, make notes about the ideas while they are fresh in your mind. (Always keep a pencil and some notepaper or cards by your bed.) Then go back to sleep.

Reverse Brainstorming. This method may be done in groups or solo. If you want to improve a technique or a product, list everything wrong with it that you or a group can think of. Then take each wrong thing and brainstorm ways to overcome it.

Visualizing the Solution. Write down in one or two sentences the conditions that will exist when the problem is solved. Concentrate affirmatively on how to bring about those conditions, rather than concentrating negatively on the problem.

The W_5H Formula. Apply Who, What, Where, When, Why, and How to the problem and then to the solution. For example:

PROBLEM		SOLUTION
Employees	*Who*	Employees
20- to 30-minute coffee breaks	*What*	15-minute coffee breaks
In the lunchroom	*Where*	Not in lunchroom—around a canteen in some central location
Morning break time	*When*	Morning break time
Socializing	*Why*	To minimize socializing at break time; open lunchroom from 7:30 to 8:00 A.M. for rolls, coffee, and socializing.
Seated at tables	*How*	Standing up

Looking for Alternatives. If a system or procedure doesn't work, apply the W_5H formula to think of alternatives. For example:

PROBLEM

Who	Mailroom personnel
What	Outgoing mail not ready for mail pickup

Where	In various departments of offices
When	Afternoon pickup
Why	Pickup too early
How	Office personnel bring mail to mailroom after mail pickup—time wasted

ALTERNATE NO. 1

Who	Mailroom personnel
What	Outgoing mail ready for pickup
Where	Various departments and offices
When	Afternoon pickup
Why	Picked up later
How	Add more mailroom personnel to process mail in less time

ALTERNATE NO. 2

Who	Mailroom personnel
What	Outgoing mail ready for pickup
Where	Various departments and offices
When	Afternoon pickup
Why	Pick up at same time as now
How	U.S. mail truck arrive at building later to allow mailroom personnel more time to process mail

Profit and Loss Testing.   Often tasks that once had a purpose are continued long after there is no need for them. Or, steps have been added to what was once a simple procedure until it has become a complicated, time-consuming operation. Test the value of tasks and each step of a procedure by asking:

- ▶ Why do we do it?
- ▶ What do we profit by doing it?
- ▶ What would we lose if we didn't do it?
- ▶ Would we profit more by doing it differently?

SOME DOS AND DON'TS OF DECISION MAKING

1. Don't avoid making a decision by having a committee study the problem.
2. Do define the problem before you start; but

3. Don't become a victim of analysis paralysis.
4. Don't let prejudices, favoritism, or bias slow your decision making.
5. Do use the decision-making technique that best fits the problem.
6. Don't jump to conclusions or make assumptions.
7. Do consider opposing viewpoints.
8. Do verify facts and distinguish between fact and opinion.
9. Do look beyond the obvious problem for hidden problems.
10. Do view decision making as opportunities for your own professional growth.
11. Do develop alternative decisions.
12. Do review decisions to see how well they are working.
13. Do pray this well-known prayer every morning:

> God, grant me the serenity to accept the things
> I cannot change, the courage to change the things I
> can, and the wisdom to know the difference.

6

A Time
to Write

CLEAR COMPOSITION

Clear composition conserves the time of both the writer and the reader. As you form the habit of writing clearly, you will accomplish more writing in less time. Clarity is shortness, simplicity, and strength. But before you can put these into a piece of writing, you must know your purpose for writing. To paraphrase Plato: *Wise men write because they have something to write about; fools write because they have to write about something.*

Before you begin to write or dictate, an orderly outline is essential.

1. Think:

Who?	Visualize the reader(s).
What?	Pinpoint the message. If you are answering

a letter, find the heart of the letter you are answering. Underline important parts or questions that should be answered.

Why? Why are you writing? What do you want your writing to accomplish? Every sentence should move you closer to your goal. Your sentences will do that if you have your reason for writing clearly established in your own mind and you keep it in mind as you write.

2. List . . . each thought you want to express on a slip of paper or a 3 by 5 card—just a word or two on each point.

3. Arrange . . . your points in logical order, discarding any that are irrelevant. One of the main causes of a disjointed letter is insertion of afterthoughts in an illogical sequence. If you are writing on more than one subject, cover one thoroughly before going to the next.

Caution: Don't cover too many subjects in one letter. The reader will pay attention to only the one that is most interesting and disregard the rest, or will feel overwhelmed and disregard them all.

When you have completed these three steps, you will have outlined your letter. All that is left to do is dictate it with clarity, that is, paying attention to shortness, simplicity, and strength.

Shortness

Do not burden your reader with too much data, nor leave out important information that would make your message clear. Careful outlining will ensure proper length of your letter. One-page letters are more quickly read and digested than letters of two, three, or four pages. Edit for any irrelevancy and your letter will probably be the right length for the subject on which you are writing. Be sure to watch out for the following space and time wasters:

1. *Repeating unnecessary data.* If you are answering a letter, don't repeat in your letter what has already been said in the letter you are answering. And don't review your previous correspondence. Usually it is not necessary to acknowledge receipt of the letter you are answering. The fact that you are answering it is acknowledgment enough. If you do want to acknowledge it, combine the acknowledgment with a thank you or a complimentary remark about the letter you are answering. For

example: *Thank you for your letter of . . .* or *I was delighted to hear from you on. . . .* Put any necessary reference information in a reference line at the top of the page rather than in the body of the letter.

2. *Excessive qualifying words and phrases.* For example, in *absolutely complete, absolutely* is unnecessary. What is complete is complete. Another example is *misposted in error:* if it was misposted, it was in error, so *misposted* is all that is necessary.

3. *Phrases that have the same meaning as verbs.* Use a direct verb when possible, rather than a longer phrase. *Reached a decision* means *decided. Make a presentation* means *present.*

4. *Say-nothing words and phrases.* In the sentence, **It is believed that the sum of** $600 *should be spent* **in the interest** of this program, the phrases in bold face are superfluous. *We should spend $600 on this program* is more direct and saves ten words.

5. *Repetition.* What is gained in emphasis by the writer is lost in boredom by the reader. It is time-wise to make the point clear the first time.

6. *Adjectives and adverbs*—unless they are necessary for understanding the message. Adjectives and adverbs are like the noodles in Hamburger Helper: They make the letter last longer, but the meat of the message is often hard to find.

Simplicity

Many formulas have been developed to test readability levels of writing. Rudolph Flesch's Reading Ease Formula and Robert Gunning's Fog Index are two of the most widely used formulas. Many large newspapers and periodicals apply such formulas to make sure they maintain acceptable ease of reading.

Here are some time-saving ways to achieve simplicity in writing:

1. Avoid ambiguity. For example, *He said today the report is three days past due.* Which is meant: that he said it today, or that the report is three days past due as of today? Be sure your meaning is clear on the first reading.

2. Avoid technical language unless you are certain your reader understands it. The same is true of excessive abbreviating.

3. Don't be formal. *In reply to yours of the first instant* and *I beg to remain your humble servant* have long ago found their places in the archives of our language.

4. Write conversationally. It's more quickly understood. An oc-

casional contraction, as in the previous sentence, is acceptable in business letters.

5. Avoid tired words and phrases such as the following:

Feel free to call me	*Call me* is enough
Be kind enough to	*Please*
For the purpose of	*For*
In view of the fact that	*Because* or *Since*

6. If you have a choice between a familiar word and an unfamiliar one, use the familiar word. If you have a choice between short and long, use the short.

7. Write more short sentences than long ones. Few sentences should contain more than 21 words.

8. Paragraphs should be short—three or four to a page—and contain one main point. Make the point of the paragraph apparent in the first sentence.

9. Connect paragraphs with each other smoothly. Strive for continuity of thought throughout the message. You can gain continuity by:

   a. Repeating a word, phrase, or thought from the last sentence of a paragraph in the first sentence of the next paragraph.

   b. Using connective words such as *therefore, nevertheless, so, also,* and the like.

10. If you have to mention several items, it will save the reader time if you tabulate them. The items will register more quickly in the mind of the reader.

Strength

Strength of prose is like strength of character. It inspires confidence. You will get a more favorable response if your reader has confidence in you. Make your writing strong by:

1. *Using precise language.* Write so your reader can picture your thought. Don't say *a foreign car* if you can say *a 1969 blue Volkswagon.* Your reader will get your message quicker if, from your words, s/he can visualize the same object you visualized when you wrote the words.

2. *Using active verbs.* Your writing will encourage confidence if it

moves along at a snappy pace. Which sounds stronger? *There will be a meeting of the Board members this afternoon* or *The Board of Directors will meet at 1 P.M.?*

3. *Not hedging on the truth.* Eliminate phrases such as *It would appear that* and *The reports seem to indicate that.*

4. *Using parallel construction.* Compare the following sentences and notice how changing the participle *providing* to the verb, *provide,* makes the two thoughts in the same sentence parallel and increases the strength of the sentence.

The reform we seek would lower local property taxes, while at the same time *providing* our students with more equitable funding for their educational programs.	The reform we seek would lower local property taxes and, at the same time *provide* our students with more equitable funding for their educational programs.

5. *Using positive construction.* Compare the following sentences for strength.

He was not very often on time to committee meetings.	He usually came to committee meetings late.
He didn't think committee meetings were useful.	He thought committee meetings were useless.

6. *Using punctuation for the purpose of clarifying what is written and strengthening its meaning.* Too much punctuation has the opposite effect, though. Use enough to assure clarity, but no more. If the punctuation mark will make your meaning clearer, put it in. If not, leave it out.

TONE

You may feel justified in sending a torrid tirade to someone. But there are wiser ways to vent anger, such as a workout in the gym, pounding your desk, or jogging around the office several times. You will at least have gained some benefits from the exercise. When you have taken time to simmer down and begun to dictate, listen for your still-smoldering embers, like:

1. *Accusing verbs.* For example, *You* **claim.** . . . (Your reader may feel you think you've caught him in a lie.)

2. *Red flag words and phrases.* For example, *We will mail your order on the* **condition** *that you pay the balance of your account within thirty days.* (*With the understanding* that sounds more friendly.) Phrases such as, *We are at a loss to understand* and *As you were previously informed* indicate you think the reader's intelligence is somewhere around the fifth grade level.

3. *Negative words.* People don't like words like *impossible, can't, delay, refuse.* You can get around these words by using more positive writing. For example, *You can't tour our facility on Saturdays or Sundays because we are closed then.* (Bad news!) *You can tour our facility any weekday between 8 A.M. and 5 P.M.* (Good news!)

Yale University's Psychology Department has reported that the twelve most persuasive words in the English language are: *you, money, save, new, easy, love, discovery, results, health, proven, guarantee,* and *free. You* are *free* to use these *proven* words. They're *easy* to use and *you* will soon *discover* that people *love* them. Using them *results* in wise time management, because they *guarantee new* customers and *money saved.* They will even improve your *health.*

EMPHASIS

When writing or dictating a letter you may want to emphasize a specific point. Here are some ways you can make that point stand out and grasp the reader's attention:

- ▶ Put it in a simple sentence.
- ▶ Put it in the active voice.
- ▶ Put it in a one-sentence paragraph.
- ▶ Begin with it and end with it.
- ▶ Use specific, concrete nouns.
- ▶ Tabulate it.
- ▶ Make it the subject of the sentence.
- ▶ Apply the imperative mood.
- ▶ Say it's important.
- ▶ Repeat it.
- ▶ Tie it in with the reader's name.

At other times you will want to de-emphasize an idea. Perhaps you must tell the reader something that the reader will not be happy about. Here are some ways to tactfully de-emphasize the bad news:

▶ Express a wish or probability (subjunctive mood):

I wish I could attend the meeting.	instead of	I cannot attend the meeting.
If the policy had been cancelled prior to November 10, a refund could have been made.	instead of	We cannot refund your money for the policy.

▶ Use the passive voice.

Three errors were noted in the account.	instead of	You made three errors in the account.

▶ Put it in a dependent clause.

Since all employees will have to work this Sunday to complete the inventory, they will receive triple time for the additional hours worked.	instead of	All employees will have to work this Sunday to complete the inventory. Triple time will be paid for this overtime.

▶ Place it in the middle of the letter, paragraph, or sentence.

All applicants are required to take a medical examination before they are employed.	instead of	Medical examinations are required of all applicants before they are employed.

QUICK FORMULAS FOR BASIC LETTERS

Most letters can be classified under one of these three headings: "Yes" letters, "Do" letters, and "No" letters.

"Yes" Letters

A "Yes" letter tells the reader something the reader wants to hear. It is good news to the reader. It may be an affirmative response to a request the reader has made. Or, it may be other information that you anticipate will please the reader.

First, tell the good news. Make the reader happy right away.

Second, explain the good news. Clear up any questions the reader might have about the good news.

Third, close with a goodwill statement. Let the reader know you share his pleasure.

"Do" Letters

A "Do" letter persuades the reader to take some kind of action. It may be to pay a bill, answer a questionnaire, buy a product, or to think as you do. Sales letters and campaign letters are good examples of "Do" Letters.

First, get the reader's attention and encourage the reader to read on. You can do this by opening with a direct question that appeals to the reader's interest. Think about the subject and purpose of your letter. What is it you want to persuade the reader to do? With the answer to that question in your mind, you can phrase a question that will appeal to the reader's interest and start the reader thinking as you want him/her to think. Suppose you are program chairman of your service club and you heard that the governor would be in your city on one of your meeting dates. You would like to have him come to the meeting and talk informally with your club members. A question such as: *Would an informal discussion with some of the most influential people in _____(name of your city) be worth one hour of your time?* would make most politicians respond affirmatively even though they may not have an hour available.

Another way to get attention is by a direct statement, such as: *There are at least one thousand voters represented directly or indirectly at our regular luncheon meetings.*

Sometimes an imperative sentence will get attention, such as: *Join us for lunch and tell us about your bill that will be on the November ballot.* An imperative sentence used to persuade should always be affirmative rather than negative in form.

Second, present the facts. In our example above, you would tell the name of your service club, when and where you will meet, and how many members and other people will be present.

Third, make the request in terms of how the reader would benefit. For example: *Not only would we be honored by your presence, but it would be a great opportunity for you to tell us about the important measures you are preparing and to clear up any questions our members have about your proposals.*

Fourth, close by encouraging quick compliance with your request. For example: *The sooner we hear from you, the sooner we can get the word out to our members. We would expect a big turnout for such a meeting.*

"No" Letters

"No" letters contain bad news, that is, information the reader does not want to hear. It may be denial of a request the reader has made. Or, it may be other information that the reader doesn't want to hear about.

First, open with a neutral statement, one upon which you and the reader can agree. Suppose you are the governor in our foregoing example and you cannot meet with the service club that has invited you to a meeting. You could begin by saying: *I appreciate the invitation you extended me to meet with* _____ (name of service club). *It certainly would be an opportunity for me to share some of my thoughts with influential people in* _____(city).

Second, explain the "why" of the bad news as positively and tactfully as you can. As the governor you might go on to say: *My time in* _____(city) *will be extremely limited. I shall arrive there late Monday morning and I must be back in the Capitol Tuesday evening. I shall be attending committee hearings all day Monday and Tuesday. We will not even break for lunch, but have our meal brought to us.*

Third, tell the bad news. Continuing with our sample letter, you might say: *So, unfortunately, I shall be unable to meet with the* _____(name of club) *on this trip to* _____(city).

Fourth, suggest alternatives, if there are any. As the governor in our example, you may be planning another visit to that area and perhaps you could meet with the service club then. So, you could say: *I expect to be back in your area in the fall and would welcome another invitation at that time. Perhaps we could tentatively plan a meeting for the fall and as soon as I know the dates I will be there, I will let you know.*

Fifth, close the letter with a goodwill statement, such as: *In the meantime my best wishes are with the* _____(name of club). *I know what your club stands for and I heartily agree with the work you are accomplishing.*

DECREASE DICTATION TIME

Longhand or Shorthand?   Some executives prefer to write letters in longhand for a secretary or typist to copy. According to one government handbook on correspondence, a number of studies have indicated that the use of dictation increases productivity. Most of the studies show that dictated letters are composed four times faster than those written in longhand. If you prefer to write letters in longhand to be copied by a typist, we suggest you try dictating. With practice you can become proficient and you will find your new system displacing far less time than your old method.

Machine or Human? Machine dictation is preferred by many executives. They can organize their thoughts and express them better without the distraction of another person present. There are other time-wise advantages to using dictating equipment: (1) You and your assistant can work independently. (2) Both of you can schedule work at the most productive time. (3) You can carry a portable dictating unit with you to dictate thoughts as they occur to you.

An octopus will let go of a moving support in favor of a stable rock.

On the other hand, many executives prefer to dictate to a professional assistant. A time-wise assistant can be helpful in a dictation session. S/he can be a sounding board. You might ask your secretary for an opinion concerning the tone of a letter you have dictated. If you have a team relationship, s/he will be able to be frank about the tone of your dictation. An alert secretary can also help you when you are stumped for the right word to express a specific thought and can suggest persons who need copies of certain letters.

Help from Your Secretary

Whether you dictate to a machine or to a person, your secretary can help you decrease the time it takes for dictation.

1. Make your assistant responsible for all routine correspondence.
2. Jot marginal notes on incoming letters and have your assistant compose the answers from your notes.
3. Have your assistant prepare a draft of more difficult letters and reports for your review and editing.
4. Instruct your assistant on routing of incoming mail so that you are not answering mail that someone else could and should handle.
5. Have your assistant attach relative information to incoming correspondence. Then you will have what you need without having to take time during dictation to get a previous letter or report.
6. Have your assistant underline pertinent information on incoming mail to save your reading time.
7. Don't dictate punctuation except where necessary to clarify your meaning. Expect your assistant to punctuate correctly.
8. Have your assistant sign your name to most letters. Only classified or legal ones require your actual signature.
9. Don't read letters you have dictated for errors. Train your assistant to be responsible for correcting errors.
10. When you need a quick, brief reply to your letter, use a rubber stamp on the bottom of your letter with this message: *To save your time and mine, an extra copy of this letter is enclosed. Please use the back of it for a brief reply.* If necessary, have your assistant make copies of the letter on the office copier before mailing.

Helping Your Secretary Save Time

1. When dictating, specify which letters have priority. Separate them before you begin the dictation session.
2. After dictating, give your assistant the correspondence relating to your dictation. It will save time in looking up addresses and correct spelling of names—and relieve you of the need to dictate this information. Also, having the file will help your assistant in reading her/his shorthand notes or understanding a word that

has become garbled on the dictating machine. Also, dictated figures can be verified before typing.

3. Give special instructions before dictating each letter, that is, enclosures, air mail, special delivery, number of copies, and so forth.

4. If dictating by machine, mark the length of each letter on the memo tab.

Pointers on Dictating

1. *Know what you want to say before you say it.* If you are an inexperienced dictator, take time to jot down a brief outline before you start. It will help you organize your thoughts.

2. *Enunciate clearly.* Speak slowly enough to make every syllable clear and use correct pronunciation.

3. *Don't compete with the shorthand taker.* Don't race ahead of the shorthand taker. Let her/him catch up and wait for you if necessary. You can be a time-wise team and have a cooperative spirit. If your stenographer is so slow that you lose your train of thought or the slowness makes you uncomfortable, suggest that s/he improve her/his shorthand—or hire someone more proficient.

WRITE FEWER LETTERS

Many business letters should not be written at all. Letters take time to produce, deliver, read, process, and file. If they are filed, they continue to displace someone's time for years to come.

Letters that should not be written are:

1. Letters that have no purpose or say nothing that needs to be said. For example, a letter acknowledging receipt of a letter and stating that a reply will be sent soon. Reply *now* instead of merely acknowledging receipt. If there is a logical reason for acknowledging receipt of a letter before actually replying to the letter, a handwritten note is faster and more personal.

2. Second letters that are written to give information that should have been given in the first letter.

3. Covering letters when a business card would suffice.

4. Letters that could be replaced by a brief phone call.

5. Letters that a handwritten memo could take care of. Write a memo on the original letter and return it. If you need a file copy, make one on the office copier.

6. Letters that say no more than what could be said on a postcard.

7. Letters written to route material when a routing slip would do as well.

8. Letters written in place of an attachment memo.

9. Routine letters that contain identical information and are written repeatedly. Form and guide letters save time.

WISE TIME MANAGEMENT TOOLS

Your Business Card

Every executive needs a business card. If your organization does not furnish one, have a card printed at your own expense. Not only does it affect your professional image, but it is a time-wise tool. Here's how:

1. Many times a business card can be used instead of a covering letter. Enclose your business card with the document or package you are mailing. The recipient will clearly know who sent it and how to contact you.

2. You can use your business card in conjunction with other material to build customer goodwill. Bill Evans, Manufacturer's Representative for Cam-Lok, was getting dozens of requests every week for literature on Cam-Lok's products. He was interested in securing new customers for Cam-Lok, but didn't have time to write a personal covering letter for each request. He designed a printed acknowledgment of the request with a slot for his business card. The printed acknowledgment folds over the literature he is forwarding. If the request comes from a person he has previously met, he can make his reply more personal by jotting a word or two along the margin, such as, *Will see you soon* or *Enjoyed meeting you at . . .* or other appropriate words. See Figure 6–1.

3. Offering your business card in personal contacts saves having to take time to write your name, address, or phone number or wait for the other person to do so. Unless your conversant sees an immediate need, he probably won't keep your handwritten information. However, business cards are usually taken seriously and filed for future reference.

THANK YOU FOR YOUR INTEREST IN

CAM·LOK PRODUCTS

CAM●LOK manufactures electrical connectors and
power distribution devices of the following types:

- Single Conductor Connectors
- Safety Interlock Connectors
- High Amp Safety Connectors
- Multi-Pin Connectors (Porta-Change)
- MS Molded-to-Cable Connectors
- Arc Welding Safety Terminals
- Arc Welding Electrode Holders
- Battery Connectors
- Push Button Stations

Outstanding Safety Features

Superior Engineering

Quality Workmanship

Serving Industry since 1925

cam·lok Division Empire Products, Inc.
10540 Chester Rd. Cincinnati, Ohio 45215
Electrical Connectors & Power Distribution Devices

WILLIAM J. EVANS
Manufacturers Representative

San Francisco Office
P. O. Box 6265
Santa Rosa, Cal. 95406
(707) 539-7593

Spokane Office
Box 102A R 2
Harrison, Idaho 83833
(208) 664-4386

*Figure 6–1. Cam-Lok (Use of Business Card)

*Figure 6-1 used by permission of Cam-Lok Division, Empire Products, Inc., Cincinnati, Ohio.

Routing Slip

Routing slips are wise time management tools. They best serve their purpose if they are tailor-made to fit the needs of the particular office or organization.

It is unwise to have more than one kind of routing slip. Educational offices receive tons of published material, a good deal of which is routed from one office to another before being disposed of. In one school district, different routing slips were being used for each publication regularly received; the name of the publication and the distribution were preprinted on the slip. The time saved by the preprinting was lost in attempting to locate the correct pad of routing slips. Even color coding did not seem to help the situation. When a staff member could not quickly locate the correct pad of routing slips for a particular publication, s/he would use a routing slip for another publication, cross out the printed title, and write in the title of the publication being distributed. This was a gross waste of time. Publications were being lost, getting backlogged in some offices, and bypassing others. If a staff member wanted to refer back to an article s/he had read earlier, no one knew where to find the publication in question. Many publications that were of no use to the organization were being filed, while others containing valuable reference material were lost. The problem was solved when a single routing slip was devised for all publications.

Figure 6–2 is a suggested routing slip. You may find it useful as is, or you may want to change it to fit your specific needs. The following ideas were found to alleviate most of the problems faced by organizations that have a great deal of material to route:

1. Routing slips can be printed on carbon-treated paper or padded with carbons. The office of origin keeps a copy of the routing slip until the item has made its rounds or has been disposed of.

2. Eight-and-a-half by eleven paper provides plenty of space for routing and comments. Filing is made easier by standard size paper.

3. Routing slip should carry a description of the item being routed in case the slip gets torn from the item. The description should contain name, date, and source of the item.

4. The slip should show the name of the person who routed it and the date routed.

5. A column for priority order of routing will facilitate proper circulation.

6. Routing slips should be addressed to specific persons, rather

```
                        ROUTING SLIP FOR

                American Tool and Diemakers Journal
                      (name of item being routed)

          August 19__                        A.A.T.& D.
       (date of item being routed)            (source)

   From:    R. J. Smith          Date routed:    Aug. 1,


   To:  Priority |            | Initial |  Date Forwarded
          1      |   Bob      |  B.F.   |   Aug. 5
          1.1    |   Geri     |  G.W.   |   Aug. 6
          1.2    |   Mel      |  M.S.   |   Aug. 6
          2      |   Bruce    |  B.B.   |   8/7
          2.1    |   Oscar    |  O.S.   |   8/19

          3      |   Ed       |  E.S.   |   Aug. 11



   Last one:  Return routing slip to office of origin.
              Send attachment to:    Foreman's Office
              File:_____ Destroy:_____
   --------------------------------------------------------------
   Comments:




                            (use back of page if necessary)
```

Figure 6–2. Routing Slip

than to office or department. This system pins down responsibility for action.

7. Several spaces should follow the person's name for write-ins. Someone who reads the document may want one of his/her subordinates to read it also.

8. After reading the slip, the person can initial it in a box placed after the name for that purpose.

9. There should be a line after each routee for date s/he passed the item on to the next person.

10. A statement can indicate disposition of the item after it has completed its rounds. This might be, *Return to* [*name of department*] or *File* or *Destroy*.

11. A "comments" space may be used by anyone to draw attention to certain page numbers or other features of the item being routed.

12. When the item has completed its tour, the routing slip should be detached from the item and returned to its office of origin.

13. The office of origin keeps the routing slip after it is returned. This is a record as to: (1) who has seen the item; (2) the final disposition of the item (whether it was filed and where, or destroyed); and (3) how long an individual kept an item before sending it on. A study of returned routing slips over a period of time may be documentation of where bottlenecks are occurring.

In Figure 6–2, R. J. Smith had the August issue of the American Tool and Die Makers Journal and on August 1 he routed it to: (1) Bob, (2) Bruce, and (3) Ed. Knowing that Bob, Bruce, and Ed might want others in their departments to see it, R. J. Smith left several spaces between each name. When Bob received the journal he wanted Geri and Mel in his department to see it also before it was sent on to Bruce. So Bob added Geri's and Mel's names to the routing slip, placing them before Bruce's name and numbering them: 1.1 for Geri and 1.2 for Mel. Bob then passed the journal on to Geri. Geri passed it to Mel. When Mel was finished with it he sent it to the next person on the list: (2) Bruce. Bruce wanted Oscar in his department to see it before it went on to Ed. So Bruce added Oscar's name to the list as 2.1 (to follow Bruce and precede Ed), and then passed the journal on to Oscar. When Oscar was finished with it he sent it on to the next person: (3) Ed. When Ed was finished with the journal, he removed the routing slip and returned it to R. J. Smith. He sent the journal to the Foreman's Office.

If Bob had wanted Geri and Mel to see the journal but had not wanted to delay Bruce's and Ed's seeing it, he could have added Geri's and Mel's names following Ed's name, numbering them 3.1 and 3.2.

Attachment Memo

You have probably seen vacation postcards that list all the usual statements vacationers write when they send cards home to friends and

relatives. All the card sender has to do is check the appropriate statements, address the card, stamp, and mail it. While not so humorous, the
attachment memo is based on the same principle. It is time-wise to use
preprinted attachment memos. See Figure 6–3. The preprinted attach-

ATTACHMENT MEMO

Subject: _____ Date: _____

To: _____ From: _____

For: Approval ◯   Information ◯   Place on agenda for:

   Initial ◯   Comments ◯   Discussion/Action ___

   Signature ◯   File ◯   Board _____(date)

   Staff _____(date)

   Draft reply ◯   Other _____

   Take action ◯   _____(date)

   See me ◯

   Check out and report to me ◯   Proofread ◯

Message: Reply:

Figure 6–3. Attachment Memo

ment memo should be on 8½ by 11, carbon-treated paper. Here's how to use the attachment memo:

1. Make an original and two copies.
2. Check the appropriate boxes and, if it is an agenda item, enter the date of the meeting on the appropriate line.
3. If something more needs to be said, write or type a message in the space provided. Don't defeat its purpose by using your time to dictate and a stenographer's time to transcribe. If your message is so long that it cannot be handwritten in the space provided on the form, it might be better to transmit it via letter, interoffice memorandum, or phone call.
4. Send the original and one copy to the addressee, who will reply, if necessary, on the original and keep the copy. If it is not necessary to reply, s/he will discard the original.

Letter Repository

If many of the letters you send out say the same thing, set up a letter repository. A letter repository is a system for depositing and using form letters, guide letters, and guide paragraphs.

Form Letters.   Form letters are complete reprinted letters. The typist has only to fill in the date, name and address, salutation if any, and possibly a blank space or two in the body of the letter.
Advantage: Saves dictation, transcription, and typing time.

Guide Letters.   Guide letters are complete letters but not preprinted. They can be changed to fit the occasion.
Advantage: Saves dictation and transcription time.

Guide Paragraphs.   Guide paragraphs are paragraphs that are fitted into letters. A complete letter could be compiled of several guide paragraphs. Or, an executive might dictate a letter to a certain point and then instruct the professional assistant to insert guide paragraph No. 6, for example. Guide paragraphs are often used in legal documents and in reports.

Advantages of a Letter Repository.   In most organizations there are times when a form letter or a guide letter can be used. Preprinted and preapproved messages and paragraphs can replace from 80 to 90 percent of individually written letters in offices with large correspondence workloads. Other time-wise advantages of using form and guide letters are:

1. Better-written letters. Use enough time to compose one well-worded letter and you will not have to displace time later composing many hastily written letters on the same subject.
2. Prompter replies. If the answer to an inquiry is already composed, you can send out replies sooner than if you had to compose each one individually.
3. No rewritten letters. If others on your staff compose letters for your signature, fewer letters will have to be rewritten to meet your standard.
4. Correct statement of policy. If others on your staff use the letter repository, you can be assured they are interpreting organizational policy correctly.
5. Less time used for dictating and transcribing.
6. Fewer copies. There is no need to make copies of repository letters. A notation that *Letter No. — was sent on* [*date*] is all that is necessary.
7. Lower cost. Time saved is money saved.

Some people are skeptical about "canned" letters. They feel they are too impersonal and therefore do not get the attention an original, individual letter gets. Their argument may be valid depending on the purpose of the letter. There are situations where form or guide letters are not suitable. But where the same information is sent out time and time again, it is neither time-wise nor money-wise to dictate a new letter each time.

The insertion of addressee's name in guide letters and guide paragraphs will give your routine letters a touch of originality even though they are repository letters.

If your office has memory typewriters, even your form letters can look like originals.

An excellent guide for setting up a letter repository using form and guide letters can be obtained from the United States National Archives and Records Service. Write to: Superintendent of Documents, U.S. Government Printing Office, Washington, D.C. 20402. Ask for *Managing Correspondence: Form and Guide Letters, Stock No. 2203-00903.* The cost is nominal.

7

A Time
to Converse

A survey among business executives around the world concluded that the world's most common time wasters are the telephone, drop-in visitors, and meetings. No one can deny these are time displacers. But we say they are time wasters only when they displace a disproportionate amount of time. When they displace more of your time than you believe they are worth in any given situation, you are engaging in unwise use of time. This chapter will give you practical suggestions for cutting down on the amount of time conversation displaces from your daily time allotment.

Conversation consists of two parts: talking and listening. Listening is as important, if not more so, than speaking. Approximately 70 percent of your workday is spent in communicating, and 45 percent of that is spent in listening, according to a University of Minnesota study. "Know how to listen," said Plutarch, "and you can learn even from those who speak badly." Wise listening is wise use of time.

CONVERSATION: TALKING AND PERCEIVING

Listening is more than hearing: it is perceiving. All you need in order to hear is a pair of ears. To perceive you need not only ears, but eyes, heart, and mind. Webster defines "perceive" as to attain knowledge through the senses.

People tend to perceive different people in different ways. For example, we listen to a spouse differently than we listen to a business or professional colleague. We listen to a colleague differently than we listen to a customer or a client. We do this because we have varying motives for listening.

Perceiving is not accomplished solely through *what* is said. How it is said, what is left unsaid, and other nonverbal aspects all contribute to the message you receive.

TEN QUICK WAYS TO PERCEIVE A PERSON

Perceiving a person, no matter who it is, will displace less of your time if you observe the following suggestions.

1. Give undivided attention. Don't be thinking of something else while the person is speaking.
2. Don't hurry the speaker by looking annoyed, glancing at the clock, or shuffling papers on your desk.
3. Don't react negatively to unpleasant news. It is hard for a person to say what you don't want to hear if you show a negative reaction. Although unpleasant, it may be extremely important news for you to have.
4. Avoid reading into the message something that is not there. One executive encouraged his office staff to make suggestions and to comment on anything pertaining to the business of the office. "We're a team," he said, "let's work together and if you have a suggestion for improving any part of our operation, let's discuss it." But when someone did make a suggestion, he

would become defensive and take the suggestion as personal criticism against him or his secretary. Soon the suggestions ceased and vital communication between this executive and the rest of his staff was blocked.

5. Be patient with the slow speaker. Give the speaker time to get it out. Help by indicating interest and understanding, by restating in your own words what is said, by acknowledging that the person's feelings are reasonable, and by encouraging him/her to continue.

6. Don't allow the speaker to ramble. Gently but firmly direct the conversation back to the subject.

7. Don't get snarled by minor facts. Pay attention to the overall gist of the conversation. Listen for key thoughts.

8. Jot down notes of important facts to remember (dates, figures, etc.).

9. If the speaker is giving you detailed instructions, make notes. Don't rely on your memory even if you listen well.

10. Don't let your mind wander to what you are going to say when the speaker is through.

RULES FOR WISE LISTENING TO A PLATFORM SPEAKER

1. Concentrate on the speaker. Listen for how the speaker has organized his/her thoughts. If the speaker doesn't seem to have an organized plan, make one for yourself. As you make notes, put them under separate headings that seem right to you.

2. Make notes in outline form. Don't attempt to take down everything a speaker says. Listen a lot and write a little. Listen for key points and write them down. Leave plenty of space between key points to go back and fill in the speaker's afterthoughts in their logical places.

3. Avoid daydreaming. When your attention begins to wander, bring it back by active listening. Anticipate the speaker's next point, think of examples to illustrate the speaker's points. Decide in your own mind whether you agree or disagree. Write down questions you will ask the speaker if there is to be a question and answer period following the address. The Audience Participation sheet, Figure 7–1, is a time-wise tool to use when listening to a speaker. In the left column write the speaker's name. If it is a panel discussion, list each speaker's name. In the next column, write the questions you want to ask the speaker. Use the third column to write points you can add if there is to be a discussion period following the speech. In the

AUDIENCE PARTICIPATION			
Person(s) Reporting	Questions	Points to add	Remember

Figure 7–1. Audience Participation

last column write information the speaker has given that you especially want to remember.

4. Avoid paying attention to distractions. Don't allow yourself to be distracted by noise, latecomers, whispering in the audience, the speaker's appearance, mannerisms, or voice. Concentrate on the content of the speech.

HOW BIG IS YOUR SMALL TALK?

Wise men talk because they have something to say; fools because they have to say something.—Plato

We have said conversing has two parts: talking and perceiving. Talking, too, can be used to earn time dividends from every minute of the workday it displaces. The first step is to analyze how much you talk and what kind of talking you do.

Many hours are displaced out of the work week by something we call "human relations." Good human relations must be maintained at all costs. And so hours are spent—in five, ten, or fifteen-minute segments or longer—being friendly, trying not to offend, building good will, having coffee with Joe, not excluding Mary, giving advice, asking advice, explaining our actions, predicting the weather, discussing sports, and so on and on and on. Good relations *are* important in your business or profession, but they can be established and maintained in much less time than is normally allotted for that purpose.

For one week keep a log of how much time you spend talking, excluding scheduled appointments and conferences. Use the time tool in Figure 7–2. At the end of the week, you may be surprised how much time has slipped out of your day without leaving anything of value in its place. It's not how much you talk: It's how much value there is in what you say.

HOW TO MANAGE CONVERSATION

B. J. had no sooner returned to his office after an impromptu conversation in the hall with Ms. Lillipont when he remembered something very important he had intended to discuss with her that day. "Now I'll have to go ahead and have Jill set up some time on my calendar for Ms. Lillipont—and once she gets in, I'll never be able to get her to leave. . . . Jill!"

B. J. had failed to observe the first of ten time-wise rules for managing conversation.

Rule 1: Keep a small notebook with you at all times. You can index it with key persons' names. Jot down in this notebook subjects you want to discuss with any of these people. Look at it several times during the day and whenever you leave your office. Then, when you meet one of these people unexpectedly, you can make the meeting worthwhile by

		HOW BIG IS MY SMALL TALK?					
Date	Talked to	Initiated by		How long?	What was Accomplished?	Pay-Off	
		Myself	Others			Lo	Hi

Figure 7–2. How Big Is Your Small Talk

accomplishing one of your objectives. If it's not possible to complete the business right then, you could at least set up a time to do so. In your notebook make a note of the outcome of any discussion or appointment made as a reminder to you when you return to your office.

Rule 2: When you have a complaint, grumble (if you must) to someone who can do something about it. If the electric company has turned off your hydro power even though you have paid your bill and saved on energy, griping to the milkman won't get your lights on. Yet some people are prone to be just as ridiculous in their business and professional lives. Switchboard operators can tell you how often they have been chewed out for something they had nothing to do with and knew nothing about! Taking out your frustrations on any available person is an unproductive way to displace time from your workday and from the workday of others. Low-key muttering about conditions to anyone who will listen is also a wasteful displacement of time.

Rule 3: Know what you want to say, say it, and omit everything else. Nonedited conversation is the cause of rambling, forgetting the point, never coming to the point, repeating the same thing over and over. Abraham Lincoln once said of an acquaintance, "He can compress the most words into the smallest ideas of any man I ever met." Watch out for overdetailing in your conversation. Stick to your main point with only enough detail to make the point understood.

Rule 4: Organize your thoughts. If a conversation is not impromptu, take time to jot down on a 3 by 5 card key words to help you present your thoughts in logical order without overlooking important points. Practice doing this whenever you know you are going to converse with someone and soon you will be able to organize your thinking mentally in impromptu situations.

Rule 5: Visualize your ideas for other people. Many people can grasp an abstract idea more quickly if they can relate it to something they can see. Sketch pie charts, stick figures, and action arrows. Your words, too, can draw pictures. Use concrete words. Don't say, "Jane is a good worker." *Good* is too abstract. How is Jane good? Your listener's idea of what *good* is may be quite different from yours.

Rule 6: Discuss, but don't argue. If the point of your conversation is to persuade someone to your point of view, you will arrive at your goal sooner if you keep your conversation factual, objective, and impersonal. Always attack the issue, not the person.

Rule 7: Check your tone. It is not what you say, but how you say it that determines the result of your conversation. Hours can be lost through misunderstanding, not of the words that were spoken, but of the tone or manner in which they were said. In conversation what is said *between the lines* is more quickly understood than the actual words that are spoken.

Rule 8: Make and maintain contact with your listeners. Practice developing empathy for those with whom you speak. Think of each person as an individual, not as a member of a certain occupation, minority, religion, or sex. Don't let your personal prejudices regarding specific groups of people get in the way of your understanding the individual. James T. McCay says, "Learn to make and maintain contact when you speak and you will gain a rich return in time."[1]

Rule 9: Avoid socializing too much. Some socializing with colleagues can be refreshing and enable you to return to your tasks with new vigor. However, too much socializing on the job can have the opposite effect when you return and find too much time has been displaced. You begin to feel hurried. Stress builds up. You make more errors. Your judgment becomes faulty. Then still more time is displaced.

Rule 10: If possible, know the person with whom you will converse. There are two kinds of hearers: readers and listeners. Readers have difficulty following a great deal of oral detail; they prefer to see it in black and white. Listeners won't read long written reports; they prefer to hear it, with a brief note to remind them if necessary. If your hearer is a reader, approach him/her orally with the bare facts and leave your detailed message written out for digestion later. If your hearer is a listener, plan to give him/her all the details orally, leaving only a brief reminder of the conversation.

DROP-IN VISITORS

Drop-in visitors are an enigma to most executives. On the one hand there is the necessity to maintain workable relationships both within and without the organization, and on the other hand is the urgent need to get on with one's own responsibilities. If you are plagued by excessive drop-ins, here are some practical techniques for limiting the amount of your time these people displace from your workday.

1. Have your assistant discreetly screen drop-in visitors. If the visitor asks, "Is he busy?" the reply should be, "Yes, may I have him call you when he is free?" or "Yes, should I interrupt him?"
2. Meet the drop-in outside your office, if possible. It is easier for you to get away if s/he does not get into your office.
3. If the drop-in does get in, stand up and walk around your desk to greet him/her. If s/he can't sit down, you are in control of the situation. Walk to the office door when you are through.

[1]James T. McKay, The Management of Time (Englewood Cliffs, N.J.: Prentice-Hall, Inc., 1977), p. 113.

4. Ask a drop-in to walk along with you on your way to a meeting or another office. S/he will have to be brief to finish the conversation before you arrive at your destination, or make an appointment for a later time.

5. If the drop-in is a business associate, a trade-off of priorities might work. In return for conferring on his/her priority (which may be of little value to you), ask that you be allowed time on your visitor's calendar for one of your priorities (which may be of little value to him/her).

6. Observe the techniques used by other top executives you visit. Notice how they and their professional assistants manage to keep on schedule. But be selective in copying their techniques. A technique that works for another executive might not work for you in your particular situation.

7. An open-door policy is not always good, but you can modify such a policy by announcing certain times of the day or week when you are available for drop-ins. One administrator reserves two hours on Tuesday mornings for staff members to drop in if they have a matter to discuss. If no one shows up, the administrator uses the time to catch up on paperwork.

8. Encourage the use of the telephone and written notes when personal contact is not necessary.

9. Let staff members know that you require, before they come in, a brief written summary of problems to be discussed.

10. If you require the staff member with a problem to include in the brief summary at least two possible solutions, many of these problems will dissipate. Too often the staff member merely wants to transfer a monkey onto your back. Don't allow it.

11. Keep a clock in full view of yourself and visitors.

12. If a staff member asks to drop in, go to the staff member's office instead. It will be easier for you to leave when the business is concluded.

13. Have a file for each person who is likely to drop in. When one comes in, you will already have for discussion some items *you* want to discuss.

14. Establish a time limit with your drop-in when s/he arrives. When someone drops in, say how much time you have available and ask if that is enough. If it isn't, ask your visitor to set up an appointment when you can give him/her more time.

15. If the visitor's conversation seems to be drifting and avoiding the issue s/he is there to discuss, suggest what *you* think is on his/her mind. If you are right, you have gotten to the reason for the visit; if you are wrong, your visitor will probably say so and then get to the point.

16. If you feel the drop-in is not prepared for the visit, ask him/her to get the facts and figures that are needed. Don't do your visitor's homework.

17. The physical arrangement of your office may be attracting drop-ins. Your office chairs may be too comfortable or your furnishings too enticing.

18. To let a drop-in know you want to finish soon, use such phrases as, *Before we finish,* or *Before we wrap it up,* or *Before I let you go.*

19. When the time is up, use a firm but courteous closing technique, such as "I know you have to get back to your work and I do too, so I'll let you go now."

20. You may have an unconscious agreement with people that it is okay for them to drop in. It may have started with one or two people and at that time it *was* okay. But now the situation is displacing too much of your time. If this is the case, be frank with them concerning your time pressures and ask for their cooperation. Most people will respect your directness and respond accordingly.

THE CHIEF WHO IS NOT TIME-WISE

You may have a chief who causes your time to be displaced ineffectively. Here are some examples and techniques you can use when you are faced with these situations.

The Chief Who Doesn't Listen

Have you ever had the experience of telling your chief something and then later realizing that s/he never "heard" you? One manager discussed with his superior the fact that he would like to attend a professional conference at his own expense two months hence. His superior agreed it would be all right and the manager proceeded to send in his nonrefundable registration fee of $150 and make travel and hotel arrangements. A week before the conference, he began to brief his superior concerning the status of his work and the arrangements he had made for his responsibilities to be covered during his absence. To his surprise, his superior seemed completely unaware of his plans to be gone from the office and had, in fact, made plans for that time that required the presence of this manager.

Your chief might hear better if you follow these suggestions:

1. Don't pick a time when s/he has many other things to think about.
2. Don't catch your chief "on the run."
3. Don't ramble, but come to the point quickly without relating many side issues.
4. Don't neglect to indicate how the discussion will benefit your chief.
5. Do get attention using a casual prelude. Warm up by talking about something of interest to your chief. As soon as you feel you have attention and s/he is in a listening mood, broach the real subject you want to discuss.
6. Do delay your discussion until a better time if you sense you've picked a bad time.
7. Do get a response from time to time. Ask a question such as "How do you feel about that?" or "What do you think about this?" Avoid questions that can be answered by yes or no. Try to get your chief to elaborate on what s/he is feeling about what you are saying.
8. Do get action before you close the discussion. If your chief wants to think it over and get back to you on the matter, suggest that you summarize your proposal in a memo as a reminder. Ask when you can get together again.
9. If your chief usually wears glasses, try to get him or her to wear them while you are conversing. Studies have shown that people who usually wear glasses do not hear as well if they remove their glasses. We all unconsciously learn to read lips.

The Chief Who Vacillates

C. W. had no difficulty making decisions. He faced all problems head on, made judgments with the snap of his finger, and arrived at decisions on the spur of the moment. He was a man of action, and he wasted no time putting his decisions into effect. He made immediate assignments to staff members to get the project going with all possible speed. Then, and only then, would he stop and reflect on the whole problem. Nine times out of ten his reflecting would result in a change of mind.

If your chief has you spend hours and sometimes days on a project only to tell you "We won't need that after all," what can you do about it?

Maybe nothing—but maybe something, depending on your relationship with your supervisor.

1. When your chief gives you a work assignment, ask questions. Play news reporter and try to get answers to What? When? How? Why? Where? In attempting to answer these questions, your supervisor may become aware of problems s/he hadn't thought of and tell you to hold up on the assignment for a while.

2. Tell your chief what other pressing assignments you have and ask her/him to set the priority order for you.

3. Ask if you may delegate part of the assignment to a subordinate.

4. Ask for a time limit or deadline for completion of the assignment. Then put it off as long as you safely can. The change of mind may come before you get started on the project.

The Chief Who Gives You Busy Work

By "busy work" we mean unnecessary work. It may be posting information that is not needed and is never looked at. It could be preparing a lengthy, weekly report that is merely filed upon completion and never again referred to. It may be continuing a process that at one time was needed but is now of no value. This could be the result of poor organization or the inability to delegate. It might also be a case of overstaffing. What can you do to protect your interests if you are given busy work to do?

1. Keep a list of projects or assignments that you would like to be working on but that your schedule has not permitted you to get to. When you find you are being given busy work, pick out one of these projects and approach your chief about it. Be sure to point out how the project would benefit your chief and his/her standing in the organization. If your chief wants to take credit for the idea, so be it. That's not important. What is important is that you make your chief look good. Few executives rise to the top in spite of their support people. Most arrive *because* of the support of their subordinates. If your chief succeeds, your talent will be recognized when opportunity for promotion comes along.

2. Pick out one piece of work your supervisor does that you believe you could handle. Suggest that you assume this task so that your supervisor will have time for more difficult responsibilities.

3. Use your imagination to help your supervisor think of new

responsibilities or projects that will increase his or her contribution to organizational goals. In order to take on new responsibility, s/he will have to release some present responsibility to you.

The Chief Who Unduly Uses You for a Listening Post

Many executives use a trusted subordinate as a sounding board. It is helpful to them to "talk out" a problem. They are not looking for advice particularly, just for someone to listen. This is an excellent technique used by many successful top executives. If your chief uses you for a sounding board, you should feel complimented.

However, carried to extremes, this technique becomes a wasteful time displacer for both the executive and the subordinate. A school superintendent had many "people problems" as do all school superintendents because they are in a people business. But this particular superintendent needed a listening post several times a day. After nearly every conversation with a board member and often after meetings with his assistants, he would rehash the conversation with his secretary. When hours are wasted talking about personalities and who said this and who said that, it becomes gossip rather than objectivism.

What can you do if your chief supplants hours of your workday with this kind of conversation?

1. Listen. After all s/he *is* the boss!
2. Limit questions or other remarks that would tend to continue the conversation.
3. Make your responses as noncommittal as possible. If you can get by with "yes" or "no" or "oh," so much the better.
4. If you can go on with your work while listening, do so.
5. Ask a question concerning your work.
6. Look preoccupied.
7. If none of these suggestions works, go back to 1 above.

DIFFICULT COMMUNICATING

People can seem difficult for various reasons:

1. People who have a low self-regard are difficult to communicate with. A sincere compliment may lessen the inferiority complex.

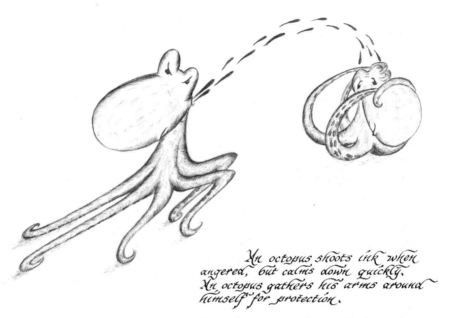

An octopus shoots ink when angered, but calms down quickly. An octopus gathers his arms around himself for protection.

2. The place or arrangement of furniture may add to the difficulty. Sitting next to the person may be better than talking across a desk.

3. A negative climate in an office or organization hampers communication. Establish a warm, positive, friendly climate. A bouquet of flowers or a dish of candy helps to reflect friendliness.

4. Some people simply don't trust others. They are suspicious that others will try to defeat them in some way. Be open and sincere.

5. It's difficult to communicate with a person who has an authoritarian personality. Listen for how your personality comes across. If it is dogmatic, develop a more flexible attitude.

6. The persons communicating may have conflicting roles. If possible, establish an area of agreement or a common goal.

7. Personality clashes hinder communication. Be aware that the clash exists and use a lot of empathy. This does not mean you have to give in, but rather that you are willing to listen to other points of view.

8. People who violate communication rules are difficult to communicate with. An example is someone who interrupts. Set a good example by being courteous. If you are interrupted, hear the interruption and, without comment about it, return to the point you were making before the interruption.

9. Some people turn discussion into argument. Remember it is possible to disagree without being disagreeable.

There are no guaranteed rules for handling difficult communicating situations. The main thing is to recognize that the difficulty exists and to assess the nature of the difficulty. If you can judge beforehand why it is going to be difficult to communicate with a certain person in a specific situation, you can plan your tactics accordingly. Large doses of empathy are good medicine for nearly all communicating ills.

HOW TO SAY NO AND MAKE IT STICK

If executives responded affirmatively to all demands on their time, there would be little time left for administering. And yet, when to say *yes* and when to say *no* can be a real dilemma. Whenever someone asks you to displace some time, remember the three "Be's."

1. *Be selfish.* Ask, "Will the time displacement carry me closer to my goals? Is the request, task, meeting, duty, project important to me?" A magnanimous person might say, "No, but I *am* my brother's keeper." That is true, and if your brother has a sincere need, by all means accommodate him. But if he is a ladder climber, or a status seeker, or if he wants you to do a job he's capable of doing himself, or if he wants you to hold an office because he has to get together a slate of officers, there is nothing wrong with thinking "me first."

   Ask yourself if you are in agreement with what the request stands for. Do you agree with the worthwhileness of it? The cost of it in time and money? Ask yourself, "If I say yes, what could I eliminate from my schedule to accommodate this request? What could I delegate?" Ask yourself if saying no will create future problems. Ask yourself if saying yes will create future problems. If you are not sure of the answers to these questions, buy time. Tell the request maker that you will have to think it over. Give him/her a time when you will have decided.

2. *Be firm.* Having decided to say no, be firm. Be definite about it and don't be persuaded to waver from your decision. It is not necessary to qualify your decision, but it would be courteous and tend to keep a good relationship if you gave a reason. If you do, be sure it is sincere and logical. And don't argue the reason. If the requester attempts to break down your reason, repeat your no and don't discuss it any further.

3. *Be pleasant.* Say no as pleasantly as you can. You may be able to

suggest someone else. Express appreciation for having been thought of. Express your regrets. But don't overdo your regrets because that would be insincere. If you really regretted it that much, you would find a way to do it.

FAST VOCABULARY BUILDING

As an executive you know the importance of being able to converse freely without having to grope for the right word. You also know the importance of speaking in the "language" of the person you are conversing with. Vocabulary needs to be worked on every day. In our highly technical, scientific, and computerized world, the birth rate of new words is astounding. Here are some ideas you can use to keep your vocabulary alive and up-to-date.

1. Regularly read business publications and the business pages of your newspaper. If you work in sales, you definitely need to know the business vocabulary of your customers. Read the trade magazines in their fields.
2. Watch for feedback from the people you converse with. If they seem to be puzzled or if you are having to reexplain too often, you may be using terminology unfamiliar to them.
3. Listen for monotony in your conversation. Do you use the same words and phrases over and over again? Keep a pocket thesaurus with you and when you have a spare moment, perhaps waiting for an elevator, look up some alternative words for the words you use too often.
4. Whenever you come across a word in your reading that is unfamiliar to you, take time to look it up. Be sure you are using a current dictionary.
5. Keep a notebook of new words you learn and use them occasionally in your conversation.
6. Watch for differences between meaning and usage. Sometimes words and phrases are used in a different sense when spoken than the actual dictionary definition. For example, the car salesman says, "We will give you up to $500 on your trade-in." The dictionary meaning is "$500." "Up to" means all the way up to. In reality, of course, the salesman means any amount from $1 to $500.
7. Familiarize yourself with words and phrases used by different

kinds of employees. Make a point to spend a few minutes now and then talking with clerks, janitors, foremen, assembly line workers, etc.

8. Many unfamiliar words will not stump you if you know how words are put together. Study word roots, prefixes, and suffixes, so that from them you can understand the meaning of new words quickly.

COMMUNICATING WITH ELECTED OFFICIALS

The U.S. News Washington Letter of July 29, 1977, contains good advice for making the most of your communication with elected officials.[2] In summary, it counsels:

1. Use the weeks when Congress will be in recess to profitable advantage. Most of its members will be at home and that gives you a chance to talk to your local representative face to face. Use this time to sound off on major issues and on personal matters—for example, to have a passport issued in a hurry, to propose someone for admission to a service academy, or to untangle delivery of a veteran's benefits. Members of Congress can help arrange emergency leave for military personnel, or prod an agency that has been dragging its feet.

2. Get your thoughts together in advance, then phone for an appointment. Most district congressional offices are under "U.S." in the local telephone directories.

3. Take along factual supporting material.

4. Don't be hesitant about showing political muscle. Most lawmakers face reelection and they want your support.

5. Don't worry if you are turned over to an aide. It is not a runaround. Most legislators use assistants as eyes and ears in Washington and back home.

6. Sometimes legislators conduct public meetings while on recess. You may decide this is the best forum for you to use. Local newspapers announce when legislators are touring their districts, and give time, dates, and places where they will meet with constituents.

[2]The U.S. News Washington Letter, July 29, 1977, p. 1.

THE TELEPHONE

The telephone has been described by a sociologist as *the greatest nuisance among conveniences and the greatest convenience among nuisances.*

Analyze the time you spend on the telephone. Use the tool in Figure 7–3 to record your phone conversations over a one-week or two-week period. You may find you are not spending too much time on the phone; or you may find a clue as to why you are spending too much time on the phone. You may find you are taking calls that someone else should be handling. You may discover you are using more time on certain calls than they are worth. You may be holding long conversations when a brief, handwritten memo would serve the purpose equally well. The average business call should take only five or six minutes. A six-minute call is equivalent to about a 150-word letter.

Put this time tool on a 5 by 8 card, one call per card. After the two-week period the cards can be shuffled in whatever manner desirable to obtain specific information. For example, all calls to or from the same

```
TELEPHONE CALL ANALYSIS CARD  _____  Date:_____
                                  (your name)

Person I talked to: _____   Call initiated by:   Time in Minutes
                                     Self  _____
Subject: _____   Other Party _____
_____    Could someone else have handled?_____
_____    Who? _____

Was call a follow-up of correspondence? _____ of previous call? _____
Would a brief memo have taken less time and served equally as well? _____
Value of call in relation to my priorities:  Low _____ Medium _____ High ___
------------------------------------------------------------------------
Use this space to record any other pertinent information you wish to study,
such as number of interruptions during call.  Did you have to wait while your
assistant looked up relative information?  Etc.
```

Figure 7–3. Telephone Call Analysis Card

person can be pulled and studied. If many of them were follow-up of previous correspondence, a need for clearer writing may be indicated.

Rules for Managing Telephone Conversation

The Ten Rules for Managing Conversation earlier in this chapter also apply to telephoning. Here are some additional ideas for changing your telephone into a time tool.

1. Instead of using separate *While you were out* or similar memos for telephone messages, use a bound phone memo book. Several copies are printed to a page, with carbon. The original page is perforated so it can be torn out and given to the callee, and the carbon copy remains in the book as a permanent record of the call.

The time advantages of this system over separate memos are:

a. Copies of separate messages tend to get misplaced. To be of use they must be filed chronologically or kept on a spike file. They are difficult to work with this way. Bound in a book they are kept chronologically, no filing is necessary, and specific messages are quickly located.

b. If the name or phone number of a person who called is needed several days or weeks later, your professional assistant has the information in the permanent record book.

c. You have a record of the frequency of calls from the same person.

d. You have a record of the frequency of calls on the same subject.

e. You have a record of how many incoming calls are being received by your office as a whole and by individual staff members.

f. Having such records on hand saves the time of having to make a survey whenever this information is needed.

2. Keep a similar record of all outgoing calls you make. Jot down the date, time, the person's name, phone number, and a brief summary of the conversation. You may want to use the same kind of phone memo book mentioned above for incoming calls. With a colored marker, "paint" the edge of the pages along one side of the pad to distinguish these from the incoming calls. Keep this book on your desk near the phone. The originals can be torn out, stapled to any memos from the same person or on the same subject, and filed for future reference. It would be a good idea to have each staff member follow the same procedure.

3. To make your phone messages brief and to the point, think of TEA.

T: Tell the person, in one sentence, if you can, the purpose of your call.

E: Explain briefly.

A: Action. Say what you plan to do or what you want the person to do.

For example:

T: Jim, we need to repair boiler # 2.

E: The pressure is way up.

A: Will you check it out right away?

4. Cut down on your incoming calls by educating your callers to phone your support people instead of you. When someone calls you for information a support person could handle, say "Jim is knowledgeable in that. May I have him call you back in 30 minutes?" Then explain the situation to Jim and be sure he calls back at the specified time with the information the caller asked for plus any other helpful information available. Soon, most of your callers will learn they can get what they need quicker by going directly to the subordinate.

5. Train your professional assistant to screen your calls. Your assistant should know the organization well enough to know who can handle which calls, and should be skilled in making time-saving suggestions to callers. However, if your assistant does not know who should take a call, have her/him take the caller's name and phone number and have the proper person return the call. This procedure is better public relations than taking the caller on an unasked-for tour of the organization by phone. Caution your assistant to be thoughtful of the caller's time. A caller should not be kept waiting on the line indefinitely. If delay is unavoidable, a return call should be suggested. If it is necessary to put a caller on "hold," your assistant should make a reassuring check with the caller every minute or two at the most. Eliminate "still busy" and "hold on" from your assistant's vocabulary. Instruct him/her to say a complete sentence, such as, "I'm sorry for the delay, Mr. Smith" or "Mr. Hunt will be right with you, Mr. Smith," and wait for a second or two before leaving the line again in case the caller wants to say something.

6. When you leave your office for any length of time, it is time-wise to tell your assistant where you can be reached and approximately how long you will be there.

7. Let your caller know your time constraint. If you have only three minutes to talk, say so at the beginning. Then it will be easier to close the conversation when the three minutes are up.

8. Keep a three-minute egg timer by your phone. When you begin the conversation, turn it over. If you turn it over more than one more time before the call is ended, the call may be dragging on too long.

9. Place your outgoing calls in priority order. If you cannot complete them all, you will have completed the most important.

10. Keep a list of frequently called numbers by your phone. Be sure also to include emergency numbers. Your assistant should also have this list handy.

11. If you are making a call and are about to be put on hold, find out who you are talking with and the extension number in case you are cut off.

12. Don't play Ping-Pong on the phone. If you return a call to someone and s/he is out, let the secretary know when you will again be available, or ask the secretary when is the best time to reach the other person, or make an appointment to call at a specific time.

13. Always identify yourself when you call or answer the phone. The game of "Who am I?" is a wasteful time displacer.

14. If you are unable to reach the person you call, you can make an appointment through the secretary to call back at a certain time, to avoid another time-consuming, unsuccessful attempt to reach your party.

15. If it is feasible in your situation, limit the time you will accept calls, say from 1:00 to 3:00 in the afternoon. Reserve the first hour of the day to make outgoing calls.

16. You may be getting calls that are prompted by a lack of information. Your business letters may not be giving enough information, thus prompting a phone call for more detail. Your organization may need to update price lists, schedules, etc.

17. Could job titles of people in your organization be made to more clearly reflect their function? Callers who are confused about who to ask for will usually begin at the top.

18. Keep a pad and pencil next to your phone at all times.

19. Have the appropriate reference material ready for each of your outgoing phone calls.

20. Group your outgoing calls. Make as many calls as you can at one time.

21. Place your own calls when you are reasonably sure you will reach the other person. If your assistant places your call, it is time-wise to stay around to take the call when the other person is on the line.

22. Your local telephone company can arrange conference calls for you. This saves the time of several people's having to assemble in one

place for a conference. If they are widely separated, it would also save on travel expense.

23. Use an amplifying device if it is agreeable to the other person. In this way a colleague can hear the conversation and you will be saved the time it would take to brief your colleague later.

24. Occasionally stand up when you call. It will help to relieve tensions and make you sound more enthusiastic.

25. Tell your secretary not to put calls through to you during specific periods throughout the day. This action allows you to accomplish other assignments without interruption by phone.

26. Gesture when you speak on the phone. Even though your gestures cannot be seen, they can be heard through your voice. Your voice will pick up their tone and inflections and you will be more quickly understood.

ORGANIZING AND GIVING A SPEECH

Here is a quick way to organize a speech:

1. On a 5 by 8 card write your major objective in one sentence. In other words, write the essence of your speech in one sentence. Use this as your introduction.
2. Write each idea you have that backs up your major objective or proves your point. Write each idea on a separate 5 by 8 card.
3. Find an illustration or example to explain each idea and write it on another 5 by 8 card. Staple it to the back of the card containing the idea it illustrates.
4. Now sort out your ideas and use only the four or five best ones.
5. Arrange the four or five ideas you have selected in logical order.
6. Write on another 5 by 8 card a brief summary of the ideas and restate your objective. This is your conclusion.

A quick way to practice your speech is as follows:

1. Do not write out your complete speech. Use the 5 by 8 cards as notes and rehearse your speech several times before the date you are scheduled to give it. If time permits, rehearse small portions of your speech at a time. At first you will need only a few seconds. Each time you rehearse, go back to the beginning, rehearse to where you left off the last time and add another

point. For example, suppose the letters of the alphabet represent points in your speech:

> First rehearsal: A, B
>
> Second rehearsal: A, B, C, D
>
> Third rehearsal: A, B, C, D, E
>
> and so on

This is a quick way to get your material securely into your mind. But remember, don't memorize words. Memorize ideas and practice expressing them—not necessarily in the same way each time.

2. A day or two before you are going to give your speech, put your introduction, numbered points, and conclusion on a 5 by 8 card, using not more than a line for each—just enough to jog your memory.

3. Now rehearse a couple of times more using only the single card. This card is all you will need to have with you when you make your speech. You will sound like the real pro that you are!

SPEEDY STEPS FOR OFT-REPEATED RHETORIC

An executive may be called upon to introduce a speaker, to present an award, or to accept an award. If you are faced with having to make one of these kinds of speeches, here are some helpful steps to follow.

How to Introduce a Speaker

1. Keep it short—rarely over one minute.
2. Present the subject of the speaker's talk.
3. Tell his/her qualifications to speak on the subject.
4. If it's not already apparent, tell why the subject is of special interest to the audience.
5. Give the speaker's name.

How to Present an Award

1. Be sincere.
2. Tell why the award is being made.

3. Say something about the audience's interest in the person being honored.
4. Tell how much the award is deserved.
5. Congratulate the recipient and wish him/her well.

How to Accept an Award

1. Keep it very short.
2. Express a warm, sincere "Thank you."
3. Give credit to others who have helped you achieve the honor.
4. Tell what the award means to you and what you will do with it.
5. End with another expression of thanks.

HOW TO GET OUT OF PREPARING OR MAKING A SPEECH

Some top-level executives, because of their experience and background, get a great many requests to appear as speakers on programs. If you are one of those, here are some alternatives to speech preparation and presentation you might consider.

1. Most common is to have a support person ghostwrite the speech for you. We don't recommend this unless you are good at ad-libbing. A speech should never be read to an audience; but if you can read it beforehand and be familiar enough with the subject that you can give it with a bare outline, gesturing and ad-libbing your own comments here and there to give it your personal touch, then a ghostwritten speech would be all right. More often than not, a ghostwritten speech is not well presented. The point of the speech is usually lost to the audience in boredom.
2. Keep a file of previous speeches you have made. These could be updated, reslanted to a new audience, and presented again.
3. Have a support person present the speech and you summarize it.
4. Have a support person make the entire presentation. If you are interested in grooming a subordinate to take your place when you move up, this is a good opportunity to give the subordinate experience and visibility and, at the same time, save yourself the hours of preparation and presentation of the speech.

8

A Time
to Confer

MEETINGITIS

Have you ever been invited to a dinner where your hostess keeps urging food on you? So you eat until you feel you cannot swallow another bite. That's when she surprises you with a rich dessert made from her own original recipe. You can't turn it down and hurt her feelings, but the thought of eating another bite is so repulsive that you would like to vanish until the sugary creation has been consumed by others. That's how many people feel when summoned to a meeting after a week of one meeting after another.

Meetingitis is a disease that overtakes professions and business alike. Meetings are necessary for a healthy organization, just as food is necessary for a healthy body. But too many meetings, like too much food, can have the opposite effect, causing a breakdown in the healthy functioning of any organization.

The Octopus seems to be able to think and reason.

Its Causes

Meetingitis seems to be a disease that is both contagious and infectious. That's why it is so hard to escape. Here are some reasons why an organization catches meetingitis.

1. Just as dessert caters more to our taste buds than to our health, many meetings are merely frills that contribute very little to the healthy functioning of an organization. People seem to get infected with a desire to meet and "talk it over." These meetings are called for no purpose other than sociability.

2. Just as having dessert with every meal becomes habit-forming, having a meeting every Thursday afternoon (or some other time) becomes a habit. You find yourself in a meeting simply because the day of the week calls for it.

3. Sometimes the contagion spreads from other departments. The Sales Department meets weekly, so why shouldn't the Accounting Department?

4. Some department heads feel that the number of meetings held is indicative of the contribution of the department to the organization's goals. But, as anyone suffering from meetingitis can attest, this is not necessarily so. Too often the time spent in a meeting could be more productively spent elsewhere.

5. Sometimes meetings are security blankets for those who call

them. It is easier for some people to call a meeting and expound to a group than to have one-to-one encounters. In Joe's department of twenty employees, there were three or four who were consistently late for work, late for meetings, and late with reports. Joe, for whatever reason, did not want to approach these three or four individuals about their problem. Instead, he called a department meeting and talked about the importance of being on time to twenty employees, sixteen of whom were never late. He did this hoping that the three or four would mend their ways. The result was that the three or four thought they must be more like everyone else than they had imagined and not so bad after all. So the meeting had little effect on their behavior, and it lowered the morale of the other sixteen, who felt they had been accused of a fault they didn't have, and wasted the time of all twenty employees and one department head.

Another thing about meetingitis is that individual attacks of it sometimes last and last. A meeting that should take only one hour may go on for three hours. If ten people attend a meeting that should take one hour but goes on for three, then twenty hours are uselessly displaced out of the organization's time bucket. Multiply this by the individuals' hourly rates and it is obvious that such meetings are costly in money as well as time.

Its Treatment

Fortunately there are effective treatments for meetingitis.

1. Have a definite reason for every meeting. Think "reason" first, then "meeting."
2. Cancel a regular meeting occasionally to test the need for it.
3. Question every item on the agenda before calling the meeting. Could the items be handled just as well without a meeting?
4. Adopt a rule that all meetings must have top executive approval.
5. Schedule meetings as the last thing before closing time or before lunch to encourage their ending on schedule.
6. Begin on time, regardless of late arrivals. If you wait until the tardy ones come, the on-time ones will begin to be tardy, and the tardy ones will get tardier.
7. Experiment with meeting away from the office to eliminate interruptions. This is especially good when there is a long agenda or if a work meeting is planned.

8. Pay attention to effective conduct of the meeting itself.

9. Train employees in effective conference leadership.

10. Plan the meeting in every detail. Be sure you know who, what, when, why, where, and how.

11. Be sure participants know the purpose of the meeting in time to prepare for it. Have them bring relevant material with them.

12. Keep a folder of agenda items and, instead of having regularly scheduled meetings, don't call a meeting until your folder has sufficient items for a meeting. You will find that some of the items will take care of themselves without a meeting.

13. Limit attendance at meetings to those concerned with the topics on the agenda. The larger the crowd, the more discussion and the longer the meeting.

14. Schedule some participants to attend only that part of the meeting that they can contribute to. For example, if a department head is having a staff meeting, possibly the Coordinator of Sales would need to be present only for the item on the agenda dealing with sales.

15. Set up a time limit for each topic on the agenda and stick to it. Appoint someone to be the timekeeper.

16. Occasionally have a stand-up meeting. This is a good idea if there are only one or two items to discuss and no writing is necessary.

17. Some groups have attempted to discourage tardiness by requiring that the last person to arrive buys the coffee for the next morning. This procedure is not effective and necessitates that someone keep track of who was the last to arrive. Besides, it may be that a usually punctual participant is unavoidably late one time. Under such a procedure this person would be penalized while another who is often late, but not the last one to arrive, is never penalized. It would be better to provide a positive motivation for being on time, such as conference attendance at agency expense for each person who makes all meetings on time during a given period.

18. Discourage tardiness by having the minutes of the meeting show not only those present and those absent, but also those arriving late.

19. Have your professional assistant hold all telephone calls for the duration of the meeting.

20. Plan ahead for all equipment that will be needed in the meeting room, such as flip charts, projector, screen, chalkboard, chalk, markers, pencils, paper, tape recorder, enough chairs, and so forth. It's wise to have an extra projector bulb.

21. Arrange tables and chairs so that all participants can see each other.

22. Have the recorder sit where the faces of all participants are visible.

23. Have a folder with you containing all the information you will need at the meeting. Your professional assistant can provide you with an agenda folder containing the agenda and all the relevant material to go with each agenda item. A notation on your copy of the agenda as to what is included in your folder will save you searching for something that's not there.

24. If you have several different evening groups to meet with, schedule the meetings piggyback. The pastor of a large church found that in one week he had to attend evening meetings of the Board of Christian Education, the Church Business Board, and the Church Council. Several members of the congregation were on two of these boards, and some were in the choir and leaders of the youth group as well. The people and the pastor were suffering from a bad case of meetingitis. Relief came when the pastor proposed that one evening a month be set aside for meetings of the Board of Christian Education, the Church Council, and the Business Board. The meetings were scheduled so that one followed the other. At 6:30 P.M. the Board of Christian Education was called to order and it adjourned promptly at 7:25. At 7:30 the Church Council convened and it adjourned at 8:25. At 8:30 the Business Board met and it adjourned at 9:30. No one except the pastor had to spend more than two hours in meetings one evening a month; and the pastor spent only three hours for all three meetings that were previously taking from six to eight hours of his time on three different evenings. The groups found that they could easily accomplish their business within the hour allotted, even though previously each meeting had dragged on for two or more hours.

POINTERS FOR PRODUCTIVE MEETINGS

Except for briefings, most meetings are called for one purpose, and that is to make decisions. To arrive at a decision implies that there was a problem to be solved. So when preparing the agenda for a meeting, ask yourself the following questions concerning each topic to be discussed:

1. What is the problem concerning this topic?
2. What is causing the problem?

    3. What are possible solutions?

    4. What is the best solution?

    If you receive items for the agenda from other staff members, it would be wise to require them to submit them on the form shown in Figure 8–1. Such a form will encourage staff members to think through

---

AGENDA ITEM

Name of Group to Meet   Date of Meeting

1. Topic for discussion: (State the topic in specific terms.)

2. The problem is: (State the problem in concrete terms. Give an example
                    if it will help to clarify the problem.)

3. Causes of the problem are: (List causes of the problem that you know
                                to be fact.)

4. Possible solutions are: (List at least two possible solutions.)

5. The best solution is: (Write what you consider to be the best solution.)

Submitted by: _____(name) _____(title)

Figure 8–1. Agenda Item Sheet

every topic before submitting it. Often the best solution will be obvious, in which case the item would not be submitted at all. Or, the staff member may know the best solution but may want to verify it with the thinking of other staff members before taking action on the problem. In any case, having the problem defined and its causes listed is a head start on the discussion of the topic. A decision will be reached more quickly than if the topic is listed with no comment and other staff members approach the discussion cold.

Your professional assistant can collect these agenda item sheets from staff members, photocopy them, and attach a copy of each one to every copy of the agenda that is distributed prior to the meeting. This will give other staff members an opportunity to be thinking about the problem before the meeting.

CONDUCT OF MEETINGS

At the meeting, if you are the person conducting the meeting, refer to the Agenda Item sheet and make sure the problem is understood. If there is some confusion, ask the submitter of the item to explain briefly. Ask for causes of the problem in addition to those listed on the Agenda Item sheet. Other staff members may have more knowledge of the problem. Ask for other possible solutions. List them on a flip chart or chalkboard. Require some evidence that the possible solution will work. In other words, has it been done before and if so, where and with what results? Or, are there statistics to indicate it will work? Can the person who submitted the possible solution demonstrate how it will work?

When the time limit for this topic is almost up, summarize the possible solutions. Call for a vote on the best solution. This may be one or a combination of several possible solutions. You may not want to be as formal as calling for a vote, but at least get a consensus on the best solution. Unless it is obvious who is to do what, appoint an individual or a committee to see that the decision is carried out.

Don't turn the leadership of the discussion over to the person who has the problem. That person may be too close to the problem to effectively lead a discussion of it.

As chairperson of a meeting, pay particular attention to the progess of the meeting. Don't let it get hung up on parliamentary procedure, unless you are conducting a very formal meeting that calls for strict observance of it.

Try to get everyone to participate in discussion, but don't go around the table asking each person's opinion. A person who is put in the position of having to give an opinion may make one up to save face. Require participants to use the Audience Participation sheet shown in Figure 7–1. It usually stimulates discussion and, at the same time, cuts down on rehashing of points already made.

Use questions to keep the discussion moving ahead. Using questions for this purpose is tricky; do it skillfully. Your questions can blend in with the discussion and not make you appear to be cross-examining anyone. If your purpose is to stimulate discussion, don't use a question that can be answered yes or no. Use rational questioning to tap relevant information. This is especially helpful if the problem is in a technical field with which you are not familiar. Kepner and Tregoe, authors of *The Rational Manager*, state:

> With management growing progressively more complex, and experience more obsolete more rapidly, the manager *must* rely more and more on skillful, rational questioning, and less and less on experience.[1]

During a discussion, summarize often. Use a flip chart or chalkboard to list points as they are made. You may find it less distracting for you if you appoint someone to do this.

When it appears that a topic has been talked out and nothing new is being said, cut off the discussion by summarizing the points that have been made and then call for a decision. Have some tactful phrases in mind for terminating overlong discussions. For example, "I appreciate your input on this problem. It appears we are ready now to arrive at a solution."

Consider a decision or solution complete only when it answers Who, What, When, Where, and How. It will save another meeting later to pick up the pieces that were left unresolved.

If follow-up on a decision is necessary, have the group determine who is to be accountable and to whom for reporting on the outcome of the decision.

SMOOTH MINUTES THAT DON'T TAKE HOURS

Minutes fall into different categories depending on the nature of the group that is meeting. An official governing body, such as a Board of Regents, would require official minutes complete enough that they

---

[1]Charles H. Kepner and Benjamin B. Tregoe, *The Rational Manager* (Princeton, N.J.: Kepner-Tregoe, 1976), p. 23.

could, if necessary, be used in a court of law to prove the action or intent of the Board. Indeed, such minutes are really a compilation of laws insofar as the jurisdiction of the Board is concerned.

Minutes of an organization's board of directors would be more formal than those of a staff meeting of one of the departments of the organization. The kind of minutes that are recorded for any group meeting will be determined by the nature of the group and how the minutes will be used after they are typed and distributed. Minutes range from being very official to being just a summary of a meeting.

Quick and easy minutes that take only minutes instead of hours to write are the result of carefully prepared agendas. The system we recommend in the next section is one whereby the minute taker can record the minutes (or at least 90 percent of them) right on the agenda with a minimum of note taking.

AGENDA FORMAT AND PREPARATION

The agenda format for a formal meeting contains after each item, or to the right of each item, the words, *moved, seconded,* and *vote,* with space to write in the names of motion makers and seconders and the words *carried* or *failed.* If it is an informal meeting, use the one word *action* instead of *moved, seconded,* and *vote,* to record in a word or two the decision reached. Examples:

(1) An item on a formal agenda:
 Approval of minutes of previous meeting.   *Moved:*
                                              Seconded:
                                              Vote:

(2) An item on an informal agenda:
 Revision of employees' health plan handbook.   *Action:*
 (Leave space between items to record actions/decisions
 that take more than a word or two.)

If a formal agenda is used, review the procedure your professional assistant uses for preparing the agendas periodically (at least yearly) to see if the procedure can be streamlined to displace less time. Here are some ideas for your assistant to consider.

1. Use a Recommendation Sheet. See Figure 8–2. The Recommendation Sheet, Figure 8–2, should not be confused with the Agenda Item sheet, Figure 8–1. While the Agenda Item sheet is used primarily for staff meetings, the Recommendation Sheet is used for more formal meetings

```
                        RECOMMENDATION SHEET


                   _____
                        (date of meeting)


    ITEM:


    EXPLANATORY STATEMENT:














    RECOMMENDED ACTION:






    Referred by:    _____
                    (name of person and department submitting item)
```

Figure 8–2. Recommendation Sheet

such as a Board of Directors' meeting. An item that first appeared on an Agenda Item sheet for staff discussion could appear later on a Recommendation Sheet for formal action, if the staff decision was to take the item to the Board for Board action on it. The Recommendation Sheet is prepared by the office or department submitting the item for the agenda. It should come to your professional assistant:

a. With holes punched for binding in agenda folders.
b. Assembled with supplementary materials pertaining to the item, the recommendation sheet on top.

c. With the *exact* number of assembled copies needed for the number of folders your assistant prepares.

Advantages: (a) Each department is responsible for assembling its own agenda items. Your professional assistant need only do the final assembling of all items into the agenda folders. (b) Assuming that the board adopts the recommendation on the Recommendation Sheet, that part of the minutes is already worded for your assistant. S/he need only proofread it for completeness and accuracy.

2. Deadlines for getting material to your professional assistant for the agenda should be established and strictly adhered to.

3. Your professional assistant should keep a Routine Agenda Item card, Figure 8–3, in the bring-up file for routine items that don't appear

```
                              ROUTINE AGENDA ITEM


     ITEM: _____ _____

     Dept./Person Responsible for Item: _____



     For Board of Director's Agenda: _____ (date of meeting)


     Due in President's Office: _____ (date)



     Comments:
```

Figure 8–3. Routine Agenda Item

on every agenda but come up once every so often, such as certain annual reports and actions required by government regulations.

Advantage: In plenty of time for the affected department to meet the agenda deadline, your professional assistant can, if necessary, remind that department to prepare the item.

THE FLIGHT PLAN BOARD

Many meetings called for reporting and briefing could be eliminated by using a no-meeting briefing or Flight Plan Board, Figure 8–4A.

FLIGHT PLANS				
Waiting for Take-Off	In Flight	Landed Safely	Trouble Aboard	S.O.S.

Figure 8–4A. Flight Plan Board

To make a Flight Plan Board you need a corkboard, roughly a yard square, hung on a wall where it is easily accessible to all department heads, supervisors, and office staff. Across the top of the corkboard center a permanent heading: *Flight Plans.* Under the heading divide the corkboard vertically into five equal sections, using colored cardboard, yarn, or permanent marker. Label these sections: *Waiting for Takeoff, In Flight, Landed Safely, Trouble Aboard,* and *S.O.S.*

Have printed some 3 by 5 project cards, Figure 8–4B, in assorted colors for different kinds of projects—for example, yellow for writing projects, pink for typing projects, green for contact projects, blue for survey projects, and coral for research projects. Build some slots along one side of the Flight Plan Board to hold a supply of these cards so they will always be handy.

```
┌─────────────────────────────────────────────────────────┐
│                                                           │
│   Project: _____│
│                                                           │
│   _____      │
│                                                           │
│   _____      │
│                                                           │
│   Target Date: _____ │
│                                                           │
│   Project Pilot: _____ │
│                                                           │
│   Dept.: _____ Phone: _____ │
│                                                           │
└─────────────────────────────────────────────────────────┘
```

Figure 8–4B. Flight Plan Project Card

When a project is assigned, the person in charge of the project fills out a project card and fastens it to the Flight Plan Board in the *Waiting for Takeoff* section. After this person begins work on the project, s/he moves the project card to the *In Flight* section. When the project is completed, the card is moved to the *Landed Safely* section.

However, if the person in charge of a project runs into a snag and the project is at a standstill, s/he places the project card in the *Trouble Aboard* section. A note may be attached to the project card explaining the snag. Perhaps some additional information is needed and the person in charge of the project does not know where to get it. Someone else in the agency will note what is lacking and may be able to supply it to the pilot of that project. Or, there may not be a snag in the project, but the target date is fast approaching. Let's say there has been a lot of absenteeism because of a flu epidemic and, unless some additional typing help is secured, the project will not be completed on time. So the project pilot places the card in the S.O.S. section, in the hope that someone in the agency can spare a half-day of typing time to get the project completed on target.

Many organizations using this kind of briefing find it has the following advantages:

1. Everyone knows what's going on and what the status of each project is. This prevents duplication of effort.

2. The executive can see at a glance what progress is being made. If a card remains in the *In Flight* section too long, the executive can check it with the project pilot. Similarly, if the project stays in the *Trouble Aboard* or the S.O.S. section too long, the executive can find out why by meeting with only those involved in the project.

3. It saves meeting time. A whole staff does not have to sit through briefings on projects that concern only two or three people. Yet everyone can be aware of all projects.

4. It is an aid to communication. A good place to put the Flight Plan Board is near the water cooler or other area where employees gather informally.

5. It encourages teamwork among staff members. Of course, some cases have been reported where help has not been forthcoming. An employee may feign being busy so as not to be expected to help. However, in most organizations that are using this or a similar kind of briefing, team spirit has increased and there has been a give-and-take attitude among employees whenever help has been needed.

6. It's an excellent way for the top executive to show interest in and recognize progress being made by subordinates. Consult the Flight Plan Board often and make an encouraging comment now and then when you see progress made or teamwork demonstrated.

7. Project pilots enjoy a feeling of accomplishment when they move their project cards to the *Landed Safely* section. Don't be in a hurry to remove cards from the *Landed Safely* section. Leave them there for a week or ten days to be enjoyed. You might even want to add a word of praise, such as *Well done!* or *Nice going!*

9

A Time
to Lead

WHAT TIME-WISE LEADERSHIP IS

There seem to be as many leadership styles as there are authorities on leadership. One writer lists: authoritarian, integrative, and permissive. Another writer lists: autocratic, bureaucratic, diplomatic participative, and free-reign. Another: exploitive authoritative, benevolent authoritative, consultive group, and participative group. The United States Navy lists: autocratic, democratic, and flexible. Whatever handles they choose to use, all authorities agree that the styles of leadership range from dictatorial to democratic.

Time-wise leadership depends on the leader, the followers, and the situation. Time-wise executives are capable of using many leadership styles. For example, in an emergency situation, an autocratic style is needed in order to get what needs to be done done quickly. The time-wise executive in an emergency situation will not hesitate to give orders and expect fast, unquestioning response. However, in a nonurgent situation, the executive might use a more democratic leadership style that displaces more time now but saves time overall.

An octopus builds a barricade in front of its house and appears to be retiring. But its size and strength are such that it is capable of adequate retaliation when offended.

You Are Leading—But Are They Following?

You cannot be a leader without followers. Leadership is a relationship with other people who are followers. McCay says:

> A man is a leader to the degree that: (1) he has a following and (2) his following is voluntary and (3) he demonstrates to people the best method of getting what they want and (4) he is the best man in the use of this method.[1]

Leadership connotes that there is an end or purpose in view, a battle to be won, or a goal to be reached. Executives in leadership positions would do well to commit to memory this verse from the Bible: *If the bugle gives*

[1]James T. McCay, *The Management of Time* (Englewood Cliffs, N.J.: Prentice-Hall, Inc., 1977), p. v.

an indistinct sound, who will get ready for battle?[2] Unless a staff (followers) hears and understands what the goal (distinct sound) is, they
will not show much interest in doing their part toward achieving the
goal. (They will not get ready for battle.)

Likert explored four styles of leadership ranging from Exploitive
Authoritative to Participative.[3] His study has shown that the more involved employees are in the attainment of organizational goals, the more
enthusiasm they show. Even though it takes time to explain, to communicate, and to confer with staff, the participative approach is by far
the most efficient leadership style. Motivation is the prime ingredient of
accomplishment. A motivated employee will work harder to attain a
goal than an unmotivated employee. Time-wise, then, it makes sense to
use a basic leadership style that involves employees in setting goals,
making decisions, sharing responsibility, and in experiencing free flow
of organizational information.

EMPLOYEE TIME WASTERS

Carelessness, waste, mistakes, loafing, poor quality of work, poor
attitude, absenteeism, tardiness—all add up to thousands of lost payroll
dollars every year. If one of your support people wastes only ten minutes
a day, in one year (based on 255 working days per year, and a 40-hour
week) you and your organization will be more than a week away from
where you should be. If ten of your support people do the same, you will
be 10.625 weeks short of your goal for the year. In your scheduling and
planning you could, of course, allow for a certain amount of wasted time.
But as a time-wise leader it would be more profitable for you to eliminate
as much of the time waste as possible. There are two ways to do this: by
example and by motivation.

Eliminate Time Waste by Example

Ralph Waldo Emerson once said, "An institution is the lengthened
shadow of one man." Support people tend to mimic their chief's work
methods. If an executive has time-consuming habits, it's safe to assume
that the executive's support staff will develop many of those same

[2]I Cor. 14:8, RVS.
[3]Rensis Likert, *New Patterns of Management* (New York: McGraw-Hill Book Company, Inc., 1961), pp. 223–33.

habits. Here are some time-consuming habits that may creep into your daily schedule if you are not alert to them.

1. Doing the wrong kinds of tasks. Periodically use the Time Record and Analysis sheet mentioned in Chapter 2 (Figure 2–2) to see what activities are displacing your time. Perhaps you started doing something a year ago and now there is no longer any need to continue the task, or perhaps it now can be delegated to someone else.

2. Failing to delegate or delegating a task and not allowing the delegatee to do the task.

3. Being tardy. Late arrivals, long coffee breaks, and early quitting times may be prerogatives of the "boss" but they also are trend setters for the rest of the work force.

4. Wasting the time of others. Peter Drucker proposes that executives ask their support people what they are doing that wastes their employees' time without contributing to their effectiveness. To ask this question without being afraid of the truth is the mark of an effective executive, according to Drucker.

5. Having a poor attitude toward the job and the organization. If an executive is critical of the organization and bored with the job, the support staff will be critical and bored also. Conversely, the manager who is enthusiastic and excited about the organization will have an enthusiastic, eager support team.

6. Having a discouraging attitude toward employees. Encouragement is to the spirit what oxygen is to the body. The will to achieve cannot live long without encouragement.

7. Not handling paperwork time-wisely. Constantly shuffling papers and having stacks of work on the desk act as a security blanket to many people who would rather hang onto "old" tasks than venture into new ones.

Eliminate Time Waste by Motivation

While power is conferred by the organization onto the leader, *real* power is derived from the willingness of followers to follow the leader. Time-wise executives motivate their staffs to follow them by fulfilling the needs of individual staff members. Workers' needs are the same as executives' needs. Basic to everyone is the need for food, clothing, and shelter. Then comes security needs such as a steady income, insurance, pension plan, cost-of-living raises, and so forth. Everyone also has acceptance or social needs, that is, the need to have friends, to "belong." In addition, everyone needs to have esteem, to be appreciated and respected, and to have status. Highest of all man's needs is the need to achieve, to attain one's full potential.

There is general agreement among authorities on worker motivation that for people to be motivated they should have:

1. Work that challenges them.
2. Opportunity to contribute significantly to organizational goals.
3. Occasions for having their special skills and talents recognized and used.
4. A chance to be involved in decisions that affect them.
5. Recognition for work well done.
6. Opportunity to get ahead.
7. Freedom to grow.
8. Possibility of assuming additional responsibilities.

Work That Challenges Them. There are goal-oriented and process-oriented workers. The differences between the two are set forth below:

GOAL ORIENTED	PROCESS ORIENTED
1. Wants concrete feedback and knowledge of results. Wants evaluation of own performance.	1. Avoids feedback and evaluation. Wants approval, rather than performance evaluation.
2. Considers money as a standard of achievement, rather than an incentive to work harder.	2. Considers money as an incentive in job performance.
3. Wants personal responsibility for work if goal achievement is possible.	3. Avoids personal responsibility even if opportunity for success is present.
4. Likes opportunity for creativity.	4. Prefers routine jobs.
5. Looks for goals with moderate risks.	5. Looks for goals with either very low or very high risks.
6. Achieves satisfaction from solving difficult problems.	6. Achieves more satisfaction from expending effort than from solving problems.
7. Has enthusiasm and physical energy directed toward goals.	7. May or may not have enthusiasm. Energies are not goal-directed.
8. Initiates actions.	8. Prefers to follow detailed directions.

In other words, what interests and challenges one employee may bore another. Pinpoint the personal preferences of individual employees and make work assignments as nearly as possible according to their individual likes and dislikes. Periodically review all positions to determine their motivational aspect. Periodically review the assignment of personnel to determine if there is a comfortable fit of employee to job. Consider modifying the job or the assignment to create more interest and challenge. An employee who "fits" his/her job is a secure employee.

Opportunity to Contribute to Organizational Goals. Bring your employees into the planning. Have them assist in setting deadlines and laying out procedures. Involve them in changes to be made. Make them feel a part of your team. This is making employees "belong" and helping to satisfy their need for acceptance.

Occasion for Having Skills and Talents Recognized. If you have a few employees, you can get to know them individually. You can know what their special talents are. These often show up through an avocation or hobby. One may have writing talent, another the ability to organize, one may be a golf or bowling champion, one a leader in the local toastmasters club, one might collect stamps while another has a spoon collection from around the world.

All of these special talents and skills should be recognized and appreciated by the people (including the boss) with whom the employee spends eight hours Monday through Friday week in and week out. The employee must have status with this "work family," and recognition of special talents and skills will help fulfill the need for esteem.

It is best when a special talent or skill can be recognized and used on the job. But if it is a talent not readily usable on the job, such as spoon collecting, at least it can be mentioned in the organization's newsletter or the employee might be invited to display the collection in the office lunchroom or employee's lounge. The champion golfer or bowler might be invited to spearhead a club or league among employees.

Does all this sound too time-consuming? Does your busy schedule not allow this luxury? Think of it as one of your high priorities that will save many staff work hours that would otherwise be lost in staff lethargy.

If you have a large staff and you cannot personally know each one, you may want to assign your professional assistant the responsibility of searching out special skills and talents and bringing them to your attention or finding ways to have them recognized.

A Chance to Be Involved in Decisions That Affect Them.   Involve employees as much as possible in the decision-making process. Recognize the effect decisions will have on employees; let them know you are aware of the effect and make sure they understand the reasons for the decision. Whenever possible ask employees their opinion in situations where you must make the decision. Keep employees up to date on what's going on. It's very demoralizing to an employee when he hears about events in "his" organization from someone outside the organization.

Involvement in decision-making will help fulfill both acceptance and esteem needs of employees.

Recognition for Work Well Done.   Never fail to show appreciation for contributions made by your employees. Contribution toward achievement of organizational goals is the key to success. Whenever an employee finds this key and uses it well, recognition should be given. Every employee should be shown appreciation to some degree. There are many ways to give recognition for work well done, but the most common way is through the employee evaluation interview. Performance counseling is discussed later in this chapter.

Many organizations receive and recognize employee contributions to goal achievement through the use of a suggestion box. Figure 9–1 illustrates a form that can be used for submitting ideas and suggestions. Extreme care should be exerted by the executive in handling suggestions that are submitted. Every suggestion, no matter how poor or how great, should be acknowledged. If an idea is impractical, use tact in explaining why it cannot be used. An employee may become defensive if his/her ideas are resisted for no apparent good reason. If such a practice were to continue suggestion after suggestion, it would kill whatever initiative the employee had. On the other hand, when a good suggestion is put into use by the organization, the employee who submitted it should be given credit for it openly. To recognize work well done is to help satisfy the need for esteem.

Opportunity to Get Ahead.   Besides organizational goals each employee ought to be striving to reach personal career goals. The timewise executive will encourage support people to have their own career goals. S/he will periodically check with individual employees on their career aspirations because people change their goals as they progress from one objective to the next. Whenever possible the executive should encourage individual employees to strive for a goal and should help them in this endeavor. Such encouragement will increase their drive to perform.

```
+------------------------------------------------------------------+
|                                                                  |
|          EMPLOYEE CONTRIBUTION TO SUCCESS PLAN                   |
|                                                                  |
|  My idea is:                                                     |
|                                                                  |
|                                                                  |
|                                                                  |
|                                                                  |
|                                                                  |
|  The way it is done now is:                                      |
|                                                                  |
|                                                                  |
|                                                                  |
|                                                                  |
|                                                                  |
|  My idea is better because:                                      |
|                                                                  |
|                                                                  |
|                                                                  |
|                                                                  |
|  _____        _____      _____     |
|  Signature                  Department            Date           |
|                                                                  |
|  Instructions:  1.  One idea per form.                           |
|                 2.  Type or print.                               |
|                 3.  Include sketches or drawings if applicable.  |
|                 4.  Retain a copy of your idea.                  |
|                 5.  Place the original in the "Employees'        |
|                     Contributions to Success" box.               |
|                                                                  |
+------------------------------------------------------------------+
```

Figure 9–1. Employee Contribution to Success Plan

Freedom to Grow.   The time-wise executive will develop career paths within the organization so that employees will have an opportunity to grow and achieve a higher level of employment.

Career paths should be open to all who want to and can achieve. Access to career paths should never be blocked by favoritism or by any stumbling block that would discourage a sincerely motivated employee.

Complete freedom to grow along career paths motivates employees to be the best that they can be.

Possibility of Assuming Additional Responsibilities.   Sometimes in an organization there is no opportunity for career movement. No one resigns or retires, no new branches or departments open up. Consequently, a staff of motivated employees stay in their same positions year in and year out until all the motivation has gradually seeped out. Instead of a staff of motivated employees, it becomes a staff of bored employees. If this boredom is not checked, it will kill all innovativeness and all will to achieve. One way to fight boredom is to make it possible for employees to assume additional or at least different responsibilities.

The time-wise executive considers job rotation as a means to do this. Eventually every employee will know how to handle two or three or more positions. Job rotation not only helps the employee assume additional responsibilities, but it gets the creative juices flowing to find better ways to do old jobs. Also it helps satisfy esteem needs and may open the door for some to achieve full potential.

TIME-WISE DELEGATION

Time-wise delegation is a method of stopping the displacement flow of your executive time on nonexecutive trivia. It is not merely dumping distasteful tasks onto subordinates for the sole purpose of getting rid of a task, but rather a method of developing your support staff.

Why and When to Delegate.   When you are running out of time and your support staff is running out of work, it is time to delegate. If you don't, you will continue to be in a time bind. Never put off a task until tomorrow if you can delegate it today. One hour spent training, during a quiet period, will save many executive hours later on. Delegate when your support person is ready to take on a new challenge.

What to Delegate.   Delegate from your daily routine:

1. Duties that can be assigned on a temporary basis.
2. Fact-finding assignments.
3. Preparation of rough drafts of written material, such as reports, resumes, policies, procedures, and so forth.
4. Problem analysis and possible solutions.

5. Routine tasks.

6. Collection of data for reports and/or presentations.

7. Tasks that will challenge the subordinate.

8. Tasks to test your subordinate's ability in a specific area of responsibility.

9. Small units of work assignments from your responsibilities and functions.

How to Delegate.   Develop skill in delegating to achieve time-saving results.

1. Consider gradually increasing authority and responsibility.

2. Set clear, realistic goals for the task to be delegated.

3. Communicate the assignment clearly.

4. Give your support person complete information on organizational policy and procedure as it relates to the assignment.

5. Define the limits of responsibility as it relates to the assignment. After the delegatee thoroughly understands the limits of authority, allow him/her to go ahead.

6. When a subordinate has the responsibility for a decision, allow him/her to make it. Resist making decisions for your support people.

7. Take enough time to help a delegatee solve an emergency problem, so when it comes up again s/he can go ahead without interrupting you.

8. When a support person comes to you with a question concerning a delegated task, don't answer the question but help your support person think it through.

9. Set up a system that requires interim reports or checkpoints so you can review progress.

10. Establish a realistic completion date.

11. Delegate to the lowest level that can do the task, within your jurisdiction. If a subordinate of your subordinate could do the task, say so, but delegate to your own subordinate. Let your subordinate redelegate the task if s/he chooses to do so.

12. If a subordinate's decision must be reversed, permit him/her to reverse it. Never openly countermand your subordinate's orders. Back up your support people in their relations with their subordinates.

13. Give the delegatee the authority needed for carrying out the assignment, and inform others that s/he has this authority. This will lessen the resistance of co-workers when the delegatee

seeks information and/or help from them in carrying out the assignment.

Cautions Relative to Delegating.

1. Resist perfectionism. Even though a support person may not be able to do a task as well as you can, delegate the task anyway if it can be done passably well. Your support person will never be able to improve unless given the opportunity to do, learn, and grow. This is time-wise delegation.

2. Don't make yourself indispensable by hanging on to all your work. If you have not trained others to take over for you, you are not ready to move up in your career when the opportunity comes. You will not get a higher assignment if you are irreplaceable where you are.

3. You are only as effective as your support staff is effective. Make it easy for them to be effective by delegating challenging tasks to them.

4. Don't accept reverse delegation. If you have delegated a task to one of your support people, don't let the task be delegated back onto your shoulders. If a problem arises in the course of doing the task, insist that the problem not be brought to you without several alternative solutions and a recommendation. Help the subordinate think through the recommendation, but don't make the decision.

5. When a subordinate occasionally fouls up on an assignment, don't make it a big issue. Even the best employee will botch a job now and then. Assign tasks where success is probable, because success is what builds self-confidence. Keep training and delegating until every one of your support people knows how to do one or two of your tasks.

Instructing to Save Time.   Delegation requires instruction in new work.

1. Find out what the delegatee knows about the task. You have become so familiar with the task that you may be assuming others know much more than they do about it.

2. Start teaching the assignment from where the delegatee is in his/her knowledge concerning it.

3. Explain the "why" of every aspect of the assignment. Knowing the purpose of each aspect will enable the delegatee to take the right action if unforeseen circumstances occur.

4. If possible, give an example or illustration of what the result will

be. It will help to clarify the task goal in the mind of the delegatee.

5. Have the delegatee explain back to you what the task is, the delegatee's limits of responsibility and authority, the key checkpoints when progress is to be reported, and the time limit for completion of the task.

6. Release the delegatee to do the task. Don't oversupervise. Instead, enjoy your newfound executive time doing more important tasks.

PERFORMANCE COUNSELING

"Nothing succeeds like success," someone has said, and this is the stance a time-wise executive takes when doing performance counseling. Too often employee evaluation forms stress weaknesses instead of strengths. To stress an employee's weakness is to confirm the weakness and lower the employee's self-esteem, making it harder for the employee to do better. To emphasize successes an employee has had raises self-esteem and encourages further successes.

Do not pass over performance counseling as an unnecessary, time-consuming task just because everything seems to be going well. Annual performance counseling with each of your employees will pay big time dividends in increased effectiveness of your staff. Remember, you are as effective as your support staff is effective.

Unless your organization requires performance counseling to be done at a specific time of year, we recommend that you spread it out over the entire year, especially if you have a large staff. Make sure each employee is counseled at least once every twelve months.

The reasons for performance counseling are:

1. To identify employees who are eligible for promotion.
2. To identify employees who have the ability to transfer laterally.
3. To inform the employee how s/he is doing. Emphasis should be on employee strengths.
4. To help the employee identify areas where s/he can improve. Again, the emphasis should be on building upon strengths.
5. To help the employee decide on a plan of action to reinforce existing strengths and develop new ones.
6. To help satisfy the employee's needs in the areas of security, acceptance, esteem, and achievement.

7. To improve morale of employees by assuring them of management's interest and confidence in them as people worthy of development.

Keep in mind the following pointers for conducting time-wise performance counseling:

1. Schedule it for an unhurried time when executive and support person can sit down and converse in a relaxed atmosphere.
2. Allow the employee to express himself or herself. Be a good listener and show genuine interest in what the employee has to say.
3. Avoid preaching or talking down to the employee; rather, by skillful questioning and suggesting, allow the employee to arrive at his/her own plans for future development.
4. Plan the interview ahead of time so that you can control it if the conversation wanders off the subject of the interview. If you have made notes on the points you want to bring out, you can direct the conversation to those areas.
5. Though the interview should be unhurried, there should be a definite time restraint set in the beginning, so that both executive and employee know how much time is available.
6. Many executives use a self-evaluation form which is given to the employee prior to the interview. The employee fills it out and brings it to the interview. The executive has also filled out the evaluation form as s/he sees the employee's performance. At the interview each point is noted and only those points where there is a significant difference of opinion need be discussed.
7. Both executive and employee can keep a day-to-day record of performance successes, that is, incidents where a task was particularly well done or where a beyond-the-call-of-duty contribution was made. Such a record is an invaluable aid in filling out the evaluation form, and a base for discussion during the interview.

DEVELOPING A TIME-WISE SUPPORT STAFF

Your support staff can save your time and theirs if you take the initiative that enables them to be time conscious.

Acceptable Level of Performance

How important is perfection to a given task? If a letter comes to you for your signature and you notice a typographical error, would a hand-written correction be acceptable? It would save time. Some letters, such as sales letters or letters to the President, ought to be letter-perfect. But when perfection is not as important as time, resist having the whole letter retyped.

Task/Time Records

Whenever you assign a task to a support person, enter it on the Task/Time Record (Figure 9–2), noting the name of the person to whom the task is assigned, the date assigned, and the expected completion date. When the assignment has been completed, enter the date of completion and the time lapsed (the amount of time the assignment actually took). Enter in the *Comments* column any circumstances bearing on the assignment, such as unexpected interruptions.

Advantages:　(a) You build a record of how much time certain kinds of tasks actually take. This will help you when you schedule similar tasks in the future. (b) It gives you a comparative task completion record among employees. You will know that support person A can do a specific kind of task faster than support person B, whereas support person B may do a different kind of task faster than support person A.

Position Audit

Make an audit of your position, using the Position Audit form, Figure 9–3. Require that each support person make a position audit, keeping a copy and giving you the original. All of these should be reviewed yearly and brought up to date. Here are instructions for making a Position Audit:

1. At the top fill in the name of the position, the name of the person in that position, and the date when s/he began working in that capacity.
2. Under *Description of Task* fill in the repetitive tasks required by that position. Number each task in the *Task* column. If it is a major task that can be broken down into components, list each

TASK/TIME RECORD						
Task	Assigned to	Date	Expected Complet. Date	Actual Complet. Date	Time Lapse	Comments

Figure 9–2. Task/Time Record

component and give it a decimal number (such as 1, 2, 2.1, 2.2, 3, 4, 4.1, etc.).

3. Under Best Qualified put the names of support persons who are qualified to do the task without any additional training.

4. Under Next Best Qualified list the names of those persons who could do the task with minor training.

5. Under Could Qualify list the names of persons who could qualify if they had major training in the task. Do not list anyone who could not qualify even though trained to do the task. Your

| | | POSITION AUDIT | | | |

POSITION: _____

Name of Person in this Assignment: _____Since:_____

Task	Description of Task	Best Qualified	Next Best Qualified	Could Qualify

Figure 9–3. Position Audit

agency may stipulate some other qualification for the task such as a specific degree. Or there may be government or union controls that would prevent certain people from qualifying for certain tasks.

Advantages: (a) You have a record of qualified persons to whom you can delegate tasks or components of tasks. (b) You have a training record for each support person, which you can use to develop even more competency in your staff. (c) The Position Audits turned in by your support people indicate whether they are developing their support staffs and delegating time-wisely.

143

Staff Audit

In addition to the Position Audit, keep a Staff Audit (Figure 9–4) listing all persons on your staff, their present positions, and the positions for which they are qualified.

In the space at the bottom of the Staff Audit form, assign a letter designation to each position. Using the letter designations, fill in the top part of the Staff Audit form. In Figure 9–4, we have shown that employee

STAFF AUDIT

Employee	Present Position	Qualified	Minor Training	Major Training	Could not Qualify
Jones	a	C		B	D
Smith	B	C	a	D	
Black	C	a		B	D
White	D	B	C	a	

Title of Position	Letter Designation
Professional Asst.	a
Bookkeeper	B
Receptionist	C
Accountant	D

Figure 9–4. Staff Audit

Jones, who now holds position A, is completely qualified to take over position C, would need major training to take over position B, and could not qualify for position D.

Advantages: (a) You have an overview of your entire staff. In case of any kind of emergency where a position is vacated, you know who is best qualified to step into the position without delay. (b) The Staff Audit shows where training needs to be accomplished. In our example, there is no one completely qualified to take over position D if employee White had to be unexpectedly absent from his position for several weeks. It is time-wise to have someone qualified to take over in each position on your staff, including your own.

Employee Career Audit

A great deal of potential is lost to an organization when career-minded employees leave to accept employment where they believe there is more career opportunity. If you are an executive and one of your support people leaves for this reason, you are the loser on two counts. (1) The employee takes his/her potential along to the new job. (2) You displace time training a replacement. If you have used the Staff Audit mentioned above, it is true that you have a replacement ready for that position. But somewhere down the line, training will have to take place if you are going to keep the same number of employees. Use of the Employee Career Audit (Figure 9–5) will help to keep career-minded employees from wandering away to greener pastures. Use it along with performance counseling. Your employee will know you are interested in his/her career and will confide to you his/her career hopes and dreams. You will discover special interests and talents you might never have discovered any other way. Time-wise, such information can save you many hours spent in solving personnel placement problems. To use the Employee Career Audit form:

1. Fill in name, title, and present position.
2. *Date* refers to date of audit.
3. *How Long in Present Position* is important because career-minded people in middle management usually change positions on an average of every five years.
4. *Performance in Present Position* is your evaluation of how well the employee is doing.
5. *Potential* is your evaluation of the virtual success attainable by this employee.
6. *Employee Career Preference* should be indicated. Perhaps your

```
                        EMPLOYEE CAREER AUDIT


Name _____  Title _____

Present Position: _____  Date: _____

How long in present position? _____

------------------------------------------------------------------------

Performance in Present Position: _____
_____

Potential in Present Position: _____
_____

-------------------------------------------  ---------------------------

Employee's Career Preference: _____
_____

Employee is Prepared for: _____

Comments: _____
_____

------------------------------------------------------------------------

Replacement No. 1 (ready): _____  Name
                          _____ Title


Replacement No. 2 (ready): _____  Name
                          _____ Title
```

Figure 9–5. *Employee Career Audit*

employee wants to stay in your department and work his/her
way up within the department. On the other hand, s/he may
want to transfer laterally within the organization. The employee
may feel s/he could advance further in a different department.
For example, someone in sales may prefer to be in advertising.
This is time-wise information for you to have.

7. The next section deals with the position(s) you believe this
   employee is prepared to handle, based on past performance and
   your discussion with the employee during this audit.

8. Use the "Comments" lines for notes on your impressions while

talking with the employee or any significant information you want to remember that is not already covered on the form.

9. The last section is for listing two possible replacements should this employee move vertically or laterally. Some people enjoy feeling indispensable and don't want others to be able to replace them. Here is an opportunity to point out to your employee that *to be ready for advancement* and *to be indispensable* are not compatible states. The time-wise, career-minded individual must be willing to train others to do what s/he does. Otherwise, the employee will not be free to move when the opportunity comes. From your point of view as the employer, it is time-wise to have an understudy instead of a clown waiting in the wings.

Job Sharing

In this arrangement, two people share the same job on a voluntary basis. In other words, two people share responsibility on a part-time basis for what was formerly one full-time position.

Staggered Sessions

Under this system, full-time employees start work and end their workday on different schedules. Employee A may work from 7:00 A.M. to 3:30 P.M., and Employee B may work from 8:30 A.M. to 5:00 P.M.

Advantages to Job Sharing and Staggered Sessions: (a) Increases flexibility of scheduling, so peak hours can be serviced more effectively. For example, if your business has peak hours early in the morning and late in the afternoon with slow time in the middle of the day, you can restructure the shared position or the staggered sessions to extend the day so that the peak hours at both ends are covered. (b) Gives the employees opportunity to take care of personal business during their off-duty time during the business day. There will be fewer absences to take care of personal business. (c) Job sharing is an excellent way to hold experienced employees who would like to work shorter hours. You gain the benefit of their experience and they become trainers of their partners, especially if two individuals' time can overlap.

Flight Plan Board

Make full use of the Flight Plan Board to keep track of the status of current projects or tasks. See Chapter 8 and Figure 8–4.

Advantage: Eliminates time-consuming briefing sessions, while keeping everyone informed.

Schedule Trend Chart

The National Aeronautics and Space Administration uses a Schedule Trend Chart to forecast expected completion dates for projects and components of projects and to chart the actual trend of achievement throughout the duration of the project. You can use a similar chart. See Figure 9–6.

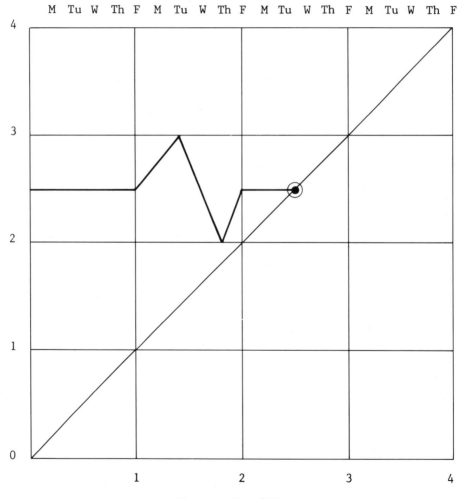

Figure 9–6. Trend Chart

To chart components of a project, show a bull's-eye for each component, using different colors, and run a colored trend line for each component.

1. Using a sheet of scored paper, mark off one-inch squares, as many as you need for the length of your project.
2. Number the vertical and horizontal lines from the lower left corner, the corner being zero. These numbers represent days, weeks, or months, depending on how often you want to check the progress of the project. In the example in Figure 9–6 we chose weekly check points. Therefore the numbers represent weeks.
3. Draw a diagonal line from the lower left corner to the upper right corner.
4. Put a bull's eye on the diagonal line at the point when you anticipate the project will be completed. In Figure 9–6, the completion date (bull's eye) is placed in the middle of the third week or two and one half weeks after the starting date.
5. Because we expected the project to be completed in the middle of the third week, we began a trend line on the vertical scale in the middle of the third week (halfway between 2 and 3). The trend line will run in an overall horizontal direction because it is aiming to hit the bull's eye.
6. Pre-established daily objectives helped us determine whether the project was meeting the weekly objectives, or was behind or ahead of schedule. In our example, during the second week the project lost time the first two days, but the next two days it made up lost time and went ahead of schedule, and on Friday slowed down again until it got back on schedule. The project stayed on schedule during the third week, hitting the bull's eye on Wednesday as anticipated.
7. When the trend line crosses the diagonal line the project is completed. If the project is completed ahead of the anticipated completion date, the trend line will meet the diagonal line at a point below the bull's eye. If it is completed later than the anticipated completion date, the trend line will meet the diagonal line at a point above the bull's eye.

Advantages: (a) It will keep you informed as to whether projects are running on schedule, ahead of schedule, or behind schedule. (b) It will show you trends (e.g., delivery of parts from a certain supplier may consistently run one week behind schedule) so future forecasting can be more accurate. (c) It will induce your staff to work towards the bull's-eye.

Caution: Don't break down the project into too many components. It will make the chart too confusing. Better to have several charts.

Thermometer

Nearly everyone enjoys watching the mercury in a thermometer from week to week in a community drive to raise funds for some civic purpose. As the mercury approaches the goal marked on the thermometer, the excitement increases and an additional effort is usually made to push the mercury past the goal. You can use this idea as a staff incentive to complete a project by a certain date.

Time Line

A time line is another way to chart progress. A time line not only shows whether or not the project is progressing as forecasted, but also shows the specific steps where delay is slowing down overall progress.

In Figure 9–7A the solid line represents the forecasted progress from beginning date to completion date, and the dotted line represents

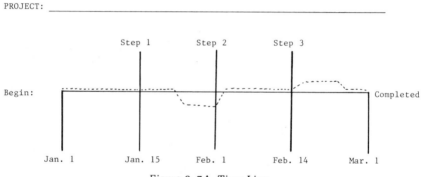

Figure 9–7A. Time Line

the actual progress. The dotted line runs right along with the solid line when the project is progressing as scheduled. It drops below the solid line when progress is behind schedule and goes above the solid line when it is ahead of schedule. In our example we chose to make the checkpoints (the vertical lines) two weeks apart. You can make them daily, monthly, or whatever seems to fit the project. Post the progress (dotted line) daily or weekly depending on the number of checkpoints you have. The checkpoint dates indicate the final dates for the steps to be completed. In other words in the example, Step 1 may be completed any time between January 1 and January 15, but it must be completed by January 15 for the project to stay on schedule.

Suppose the project has progressed to Step 2 and for some reason

150

progress on Step 2 was delayed, but the project could skip over to Step 3 and go ahead. Break the dotted line where the actual progress stopped, and pick it up again where progress resumed—not *when*, but *where* it resumed. On January 20 your time line would look like Figure 9–7B. It shows that although the date is January 20, Step 3 has already been completed and progress has stopped on Step 2. Notice that the dotted line for Step 3 is above the solid line, showing that it is ahead of schedule.

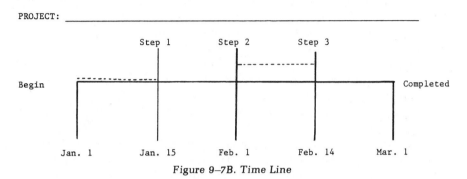

Figure 9–7B. Time Line

By February 25, the problem to Step 2 has been cleared away and progress has resumed. The project is completed on February 25. The chart then looks like Figure 9–7C.

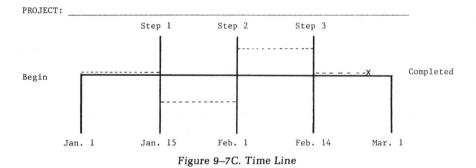

Figure 9–7C. Time Line

Cautions Relative to Support Staff

1. Overstaffing creates time wastes. Drucker says:

A work force may, indeed, be too small for the task. And the work then suffers, if it gets done at all. But this is not the rule. Much more common is the work force that is too big for effectiveness, the work force that spends, therefore, an increasing amount of its time "interacting" rather than working. . . . People get into each other's way. People have become an impediment to performance, rather than the means thereto. In a lean organization people have room to move without colliding with one another and can do their work without having to explain it all the time.[4]

2. Parkinson's Law says that work expands to fill the time available for its completion. Set reasonable time limits for completion of projects. Without a deadline, projects tend to use up more time than is necessary for their completion.

3. Blocked or slow-flowing information going through established communication channels creates time waste. It is wise organization to have established communication channels *if they are functional.* Wasted time runs out of the workday when one employee idly waits for information to reach him/her through channels. Perhaps some information needs to flow directly from source to employee while a copy is fed through channels.

4. Employees adjust to the level of demands made upon them. A time-wise executive focuses on contribution. If an executive is committed to making the best contribution possible to the accomplishment of organizational goals, s/he is a powerful force in developing his/her support staff to do the same. If every employee of an organization, from top executive to junior file clerk, would look for ways to do their assigned tasks that will contribute the most to the organization's goals, goals would be reached and surpassed in record-breaking time.

5. Every job in the organization should place a challenge on the employee. When the job is challenging, the employee usually becomes innovative and time conscious. The fact that those above feel the employee is capable of meeting the challenge will usually cause the employee to rise to it.

6. Employees must have faith in their leader to perform well and time-wisely. Leaders can earn employee faith in them if they have integrity, dedication, openness, and creativity.

---

[4]Peter F. Drucker, *The Effective Executive* (New York: Harper & Row, Publishers, Inc., 1966), p. 43. Copyright © 1966, 1967 by Peter F. Drucker. By permission of the publisher.

10

A Time
to Take Stock

SOME TIME TRAPS AND HOW TO AVOID THEM

Ill Health

A healthy body is one of the most effective time tools available to executives. Executives who manage time wisely devote some time every day to keeping fit. They know that the pace of executive life makes them prime targets for malnutrition, indigestion, chronic ailments, physical disabilities, screaming nerves, cardiac arrests, ulcers, high blood pressure, and so on. Here are some things you can do to help keep your body healthy.

1. Take an exercise break instead of a coffee break. If possible, get out of the building and take a brisk walk around the block. You

can exercise in your office. Stretch and then relax all your muscles. Bend over with your head, arms, and hands hanging loose. This will get the blood to your brain and relax your back muscles. Do some deep breathing exercises—inhale deeply and exhale completely. Do some head rolls to exercise your neck and shoulder muscles.

2. Besides exercise breaks during the day, have a definite exercise program. Engage in something you enjoy doing and do it every day. It could be jogging, swimming, tennis, golf. Get up early so you can spend some time enjoying your favorite kind of exercise. Chores around the home, while good for you, are not substitutions for a definite exercise program. If you think you don't enjoy any kind of exercise, try it every day for a week and see if you don't begin to feel better. If you have not been exercising much, don't start on a strenuous exercise regimen without consulting your doctor first.

3. Avoid a diet of empty calories. Eat well-balanced meals as regularly as you can. Eat unhurriedly in pleasant surroundings and with congenial company. Avoid eating when you are in a highly emotional state. Avoid eating to satisfy an emotional or psychological need. Encourage your family to be health-diet conscious.

4. Have yearly physical checkups.

5. Get the amount of sleep your body requires. Some people can do with less sleep than others. Study yourself to learn how much sleep you need to feel rested and invigorated.

Tension and Stress

Know the difference between tension and stress. Tension is what our octopus friend in Chapter 1 was experiencing when he was being stretched in all directions. Tension, according to Webster, is also a state of suppressed hostility between persons or groups. Norman Vincent Peale calls tension the prevailing malady of American people. Executives in top-ranking positions know all too well what tension feels like. What some don't know is how much time tension can rob from their workday. Too many people, when they are being pulled in all directions, try all the harder to go in all directions. It can't be done. When you are feeling tension because of the multitude of things you must do, let go of some of the pressures. Put them in cold storage for a while and work on only the one or two most urgent ones. If tension is present because of hostility, get to the root of it whether it is between you and another person or between groups. Hostility kept inside a person or a group of people and not allowed out in the open where it can be examined and perhaps disposed of grows bigger and bigger. Not all tension of this sort can be disposed of, but you should at least examine it. You will be in a better position to cope with it.

Stress is a strain or pressure on the body or mind. Stressful situations can develop when tension is present, when you are caught in a time bind, when progress is blocked, when there seems to be no answer to gnawing problems. Here are some ways to cope with stressful situations.

1. Learn to accept the things you cannot change.
2. Work off anger physically by undertaking some form of activity—other than combat.
3. Talk with a trusted friend, colleague, spouse, or pastor about the thing that is causing the stress. Don't be hesitant to seek professional help if the problem warrants it.
4. Balance work and recreation.
5. Avoid medication if possible. Pills treat only symptoms, as a rule, not causes. Avoid tranquilizers unless they are prescribed by a doctor. Avoid self-medication.
6. Do something for someone else. It will take your mind off your own troubles.
7. Count your blessings, not your problems.

Worry

Worry is a great stress builder and time stealer. The best way to overcome worry is to take action on whatever it is that you are worrying about. If your worry concerns a specific problem, use the problem-solving techniques given in Chapter 5, arrive at a decision and *take action*. If worry is a habit you have developed, here are some pointers you can use to break the habit.

1. Live one day at a time. You can't change what happened yesterday. You can make tomorrow better by living well today. So concentrate on doing your best today and put yesterday out of your mind. As for tomorrow, think of only the best that can happen.
2. Don't fuss about little things that don't really matter. A study was made of the kinds of things people worry about. It showed that 40 percent were things that never came about, 35 percent were things that couldn't be changed, 15 percent turned out better than expected, 8 percent were petty, useless worries, and only 2 percent were legitimate worries.

3. Use the law of averages to outlaw your worries. Some people, when they fly, worry that the plane will crash. The law of averages indicates that it is not very likely to happen.

4. Cooperate with the inevitable. Deliberately make the best of every bad situation. It is a profitable way to defeat worry. Someone has said, "If life hands you a lemon, make lemonade out of it."

5. If you are a compulsive worrier, don't fight it. Instead cooperate with your habit. Schedule a certain amount of time, say twenty minutes, for worrying every day. Then spend that time alone worrying. When you start to worry at any other time, remind yourself that you have scheduled a time for worry and save your worry for that time. Soon you will be able to control when you worry. And you will find your scheduled worry sessions getting shorter and shorter as you have less and less to worry about.

6. To defeat the worry habit and for the 2 percent legitimate worries you have—pray. "More things are wrought by prayer than this world dreams of."

Indecision

This is another time trap many people fall into. Executive decisions often are no problem. Chapter 5 gives techniques for making such decisions. But what about the small decisions people are forced to make every day? Many of these little decisions could be made once and for all.

1. Deciding what to wear. Plan your wardrobe for a week at a time. You will be making one decision in place of seven decisions.

2. What to eat. Plan your menus for a week ahead. Again, this is one decision instead of several decisions each day.

3. What to believe in. If it takes a family conference every week to decide whether or not to go to church, or which church to go to, perhaps you have not made a basic decision concerning your beliefs. Make that decision.

The Blues

That vague, restless feeling of being down, vaguely disappointed, is an emotional time trap most of us experience occasionally. When we feel blue, we tend to spend our time pitying ourselves or enumerating our accomplishments over and over. There are many reasons for the blues.

1. There could be a physical reason. If you find yourself "down" a great deal of the time, get a physical checkup.

2. Study yourself and see if the blues you experience are the low points of your normal cycle. If so, you can estimate when you will be apt to feel down and you can adjust your activities for that time. Avoid making decisions when you are down. Pamper yourself while you are at your low ebb. Break monotony by doing something different. Take a different route to work or change a usual routine. Do a good deed for someone but don't tell anyone about it.

3. You may be experiencing achievement blues. Have you just completed a big project or reached a goal? A let-down feeling often follows successful accomplishment. It is frustrating because you should feel good about your successes. The best way to fight achievement blues is to focus on the achievement. Celebrate it. Let your friends help you celebrate. Then set a new goal and get busy working toward it.

4. All-work-and-no-play blues afflict people who work too steadily. No matter how much you enjoy your work, take a vacation from it. You will accomplish more in less time.

5. It may be only a case of spring fever. Ease up a little and it will go away.

HOME, FAMILY, AND FRIENDS

The higher up the executive ladder one climbs, the less time there seems to be for home, family, and friends. It is important that you make the most of the time that you do have for this area of your life.

Many executives rationalize the time they spend away from their families by thinking they are working for their families. And in a sense that is true, but too much absence from home and family can lead to alienation of family members. Too many executives, while living at the same address their families do, live there as strangers.

A good way to overcome this alienation, even though you have to be away a lot of the time, is to include your spouse and your children in your business. Talk about it at home. As you do, your enthusiasm for your work will come through and your family will pick it up and become interested in your work. They will enjoy your "shop talk" even if they don't understand it all, and they will gain a respect for your work. They will be on your side.

Of course, you will not talk about business all the time you are home. Your spouse and children have lives of their own and they want to include you in their everyday happenings. So listen well and be interested in each one. If you have several children, it is easy to get them and their activities and accomplishments mixed up. So keep family personnel files on each member. Keep birth certificates, medical records, school records, and special information, such as Susie's Girl Scout Troop Leader is Sara Jones. Names are sometimes difficult to recall and writing them down often establishes them in your memory. Years from now you or Susie may want to remember the troop leader's name. Hopefully, she filled a need in Susie's life. Maybe she encouraged Susie to work toward a goal and now Susie has accomplished the goal and would like her former troop leader to know. Include any special awards and recognition received. Let the kids know you are keeping a file on each of them. They will know they are important to you.

Be interested in your spouse's activities. If your spouse works, take an active interest in his/her work. Get to know the people your spouse works with so when s/he speaks of one by name you know who it is. Learn something about your spouse's business so you can talk intelligently about it.

Share the big financial decisions with your spouse. Have an agreement as to who writes the checks and balances the bankbook. Share the responsibility of rearing the children. Discipline should not be the responsibility of only one parent. This means that there must be agreement between you and your spouse on standards of behavior. Too often these are the kinds of decisions that slide by and are not faced until a crisis occurs.

If you are a single parent, don't delegate too much of your children's rearing to outside agencies. Don't rely on the baby-sitter, the nursery, the school, or the Sunday school to give your child the guidance and direction that you as a parent should be giving. Maintain a continuous contact with those to whom you delegate any aspect of your child's rearing and education. Make it clear that you are delegating the job, not abdicating it.

Every family needs family friends. Plan with your family when you will entertain. If you have several groups of friends that you entertain, it is time-wise to set aside a weekend to do all your entertaining. Have one group over Friday evening, another on Saturday, and perhaps grandparents, uncles, and aunts on Sunday. You will have to clean house only once and food preparation can be consolidated. Also, you can buy food in larger quantities, thus saving money as well as time.

ONE-DAY-AT-A-TIME AND THREE-MONTHS-AT-A-TIME

Webster defines motivation as an urge to push on. If you are motivated to use time more wisely, *now* is the time to push on. The time when you are motivated is the worst time to procrastinate. Begin now to live one day at a time and three months at a time.

Use the time tools you have read about in previous chapters and some others we will cover in this chapter to compile a three-month executive time planning book. It will help you get started using time management tools. As you use these tools to manage your time, you will develop effective time use habits. Here's how to compile your three-month executive time planning book:

1. You will need a thick three-ring binder.

2. Begin with Goal Worksheets, Figure 10–1, one for each major goal. Use of this form is self-explanatory. Use this form for your three-month time planning book. If you are not going to use the three-month time planning book, keep your goals on the 5 by 8 cards or the wall chart mentioned in Chapter 1. Choose only one method for keeping your goals before you. Don't duplicate this task.

3. The next page is a Planning Guide for one year. See Figure 10–2. You don't have to wait until January to begin. Start your wise time management year with the current month. Report to refers to the person you report to concerning the project.

   Don't confuse this planning guide with the Delegation Planning Guide in Figure 3–3. The Delegation Planning Guide is to help you keep track of projects you have delegated to others. Planning Guide, Figure 10–2, is to plan for the projects or tasks that are not delegatable. Write the task in the project column and put a checkmark in the month when you will have to reserve time for the task. This will point out the months when you will have several projects and the months when you will be relatively free of projects.

4. The next three pages of your planning book are monthly calendars for the next three months. See Figure 10–3. Use these pages as reminders of appointments, projects, due dates, and so forth.

5. Then comes a series of Weekly Organizers, one for each week in the three-month period you are working on. See Figure 10–4. List the things you will do each day during the week.

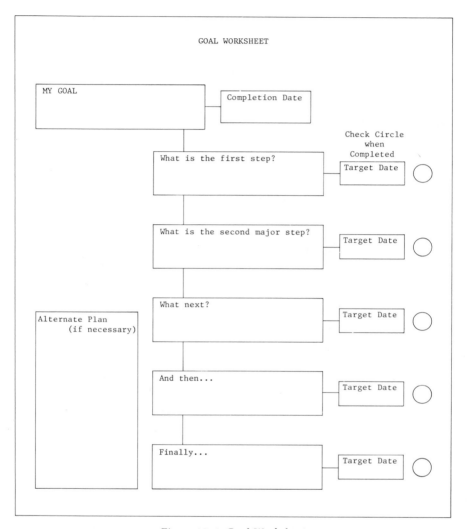

Figure 10-1. Goal Worksheet

Figures 10–3 and 10–4, Reference Calendar and Weekly Organizer, are memory joggers so you will not have to keep a lot of tasks, beginning dates, and due dates in your mind. Record them on these forms and, as the months, weeks, and days come along, you will be automatically reminded.

6. Behind each Weekly Organizer, put seven copies of your Daily Organizer. See Chapter 2 and Figure 2–3.

PLANNING GUIDE							
PROJECT	Report to	Jan	Feb	Mar	Apr	May	Jun
		Jul	Aug	Sep	Oct	Nov	Dec
NOTES:							

Figure 10–2. Planning Guide

7. Behind each Daily Organizer, put a Time Monitor, Figure 10–5. Fill in the left-hand column from your Daily Organizer. As the day progresses, fill in the right-hand column. This will give you a record of how well you are able to keep on schedule.

	REFERENCE CALENDAR					
19___		Month: _____				
Sunday	Monday	Tuesday	Wednesday	Thursday	Friday	Saturday

Figure 10–3. Reference Calendar

```
WEEKLY ORGANIZER

The Week of: _____

| MONDAY | TUESDAY | WEDNESDAY | THURSDAY | FRIDAY |
| --- | --- | --- | --- | --- |
|  |  |  |  |  |
```

Figure 10–4. Weekly Organizer

```
                          TIME MONITOR

Date: _____


                SCHEDULED                        PERFORMED
  7:00 |                            |
  7:30 |                            |
  8:00 |                            |
  8:30 |                            |
  9:00 |                            |
  9:30 |                            |
 10:00 |                            |
 10:30 |                            |
 11:00 |                            |
 11:30 |                            |
 12:00 |                            |
 12:30 |                            |
  1:00 |                            |
  1:30 |                            |
  2:00 |                            |
  2:30 |                            |
  3:00 |                            |
  3:30 |                            |
  4:00 |                            |
  4:30 |                            |
  5:00 |                            |
  5:30 |                            |
  6:00 |                            |
  6:30 |                            |

Notes:
```

Figure 10–5. Time Monitor

8. Behind the Time Monitor, put a Paperwork Summary, Figure 10–6. Fill this in from your Daily Organizer, and complete the right-hand column as you complete each task.

9. The Year Ahead comes next, Figure 10–7. Use this page to remind yourself of plans for the coming year.

| PAPERWORK SUMMARY FOR |
| _____ 197_ |
| date |

Subject of Paperwork	Action Due	Disposition

Figure 10–6. Paperwork Summary

The Planning Guide in Figure 10–2 is for non-delegatable projects. The Year Ahead (Figure 10–7) is a memory jogger to help you complete the Reference Calendar (Figure 10–3), and the Weekly Organizer (Figure 10–4).

THE YEAR AHEAD Plans and Appointments		
JANUARY	FEBRUARY	MARCH
APRIL	MAY	JUNE
JULY	AUGUST	SEPTEMBER
OCTOBER	NOVEMBER	DECEMBER

Figure 10–7. The Year Ahead

10. Personal Journal is next, Figure 10–8. Don't overlook this page. It is the key to progress in wiser time management. If you don't know the problems in your time management history, you are apt to repeat them and not even know it.

11. The Future, Figure 10–9, contains four specific questions to ask yourself. Answer these questions thoughtfully and concretely.

166

```
+--------------------------------------------------------------------+
|                        PERSONAL JOURNAL                            |
+--------------------------------------------------------------------+
| During the past three  |                       | What do I want to do |
| months, what things    | What are the          | about it?            |
| have I learned about   | implications?         |                      |
| myself?                |                       |                      |
+------------------------+-----------------------+----------------------+
|                        |                       |                      |
|                        |                       |                      |
|                        |                       |                      |
|                        |                       |                      |
|                        |                       |                      |
|                        |                       |                      |
|                        |                       |                      |
|                        |                       |                      |
|                        |                       |                      |
|                        |                       |                      |
+------------------------+-----------------------+----------------------+
```

Figure 10–8. Personal Journal

12. Figure 10–10 asks you to think through your present responsibilities and your plans for personal growth to prepare you to take on higher responsibilities. Do this after you have studied your use of time for three months.

13. You may want to keep in the back of your executive planning

```
THE FUTURE

1.  One way I will handle time differently in the future is:




2.  One of my strengths I will use more on the job is:





3.  Some sorting systems I will use to help me be more productive on the job
    are:







4.  I will spend "me" time:

    When:

    Where:

    How Long:


Comments:
```

Figure 10–9. The Future

book copies of other time tools relating to your respon-
sibilities, such as: Responsibility Chart, Figure 3–4; Task/Time
Records, 9–2; Position Audits, 9–3; Staff Audits, 9–4; Trend
Charts, 9–6; and Time Lines, 9–7.

MANAGE YOUR FUTURE

Your manager has told you that s/he would like to get together with you next Wednesday to discuss your job - the things you are doing now, and will or might be doing in the coming year. Five kinds of responsibilities will be discussed and s/he has asked you to think through these things and make some notes.

1. What are your regular, routine or ordinary day-to-day responsibilities and how will your manager measure your performance in each of these areas? Concentrate on the critical few rather than the trivial several.

2. What problems do you face in your job and what is your plan for solving them in the year ahead? List two or three.

3. What one innovation, change, and/or improvement in your own work arena and within your department do you recommend implementing and what would be the new value gained?

   To you:

   To your manager:

4. What are the areas in which you must develop more knowledge, skill, and experience? Outline your program for growth in these areas.

5. How specifically can your manager help you to reach these growth objectives?

Figure 10–10. Manage Your Future

After keeping these time records for three months you will have a better understanding of how well you are using your executive time. We recommend that you continue to use One-Day-at-a-Time and Three-Months-at-a-Time so that effective executive time management becomes a natural part of your daily routine. Then review your use of time periodically to keep from falling back into unwise, time-consuming habits.

169

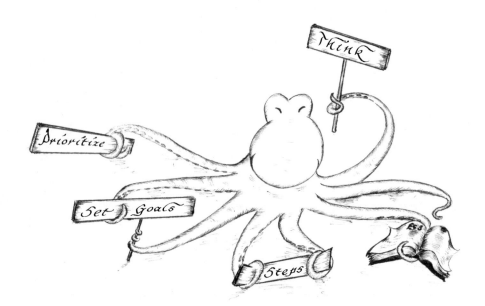

Index